big book of
papercrafts

big book of
papercrafts
40 stunning projects

VIVIENNE BOLTON

NEW HOLLAND

Published in 2007 by
New Holland Publishers (UK) Ltd
London · Cape Town · Sydney · Auckland

Garfield House, 86–88 Edgware Road
London, W2 2EA United Kingdom
www.newhollandpublishers.com

80 McKenzie Street, Cape Town 8001, South Africa

Unit 1, 66 Gibbes Street, Chatswood, NSW 2067
Australia

218 Lake Road, Northcote, Auckland, New Zealand

ISBN 978 1 84537 755 7

Senior Editor: Clare Hubbard
Editorial Direction: Rosemary Wilkinson
Photography: Shona Wood
Design: Bridgewater Book Company
Illustrations: Stephen Dew
Production: Marion Storz

10 9 8 7 6 5 4 3 2 1

Reproduction by Pica Digital Pte Ltd, Singapore
Printed and bound by Times Offset (M) Sdn Bnd,
Malaysia.

Note: The author and publishers have made every
effort to ensure that all instructions given in this
book are safe and accurate, but they cannot accept
liability for any resulting injury or loss or damage to
either property or person, whether direct or
consequential and howsoever arising.

Introduction

▼ A few simple folds can turn a sheet of paper into an origami crane or pretty little gift box. The cranes for the mobile are folded from beautiful Japanese paper and the boxes are very simple to construct.

Paper has to be my favourite material; it can be crafted into almost anything! You can fold it, cut it, decorate it, colour it, shape it – yes, paper is possibly the most diverse of all craft materials. A sheet of plain white paper could be the starting point for any number of different things: origami folds could turn it into an animal, flower or bird, for example, and, if you fold and decorate it, it could become a greetings card or a box, even a paper aeroplane!

I have a large collection of paper and have recently discovered the beautiful Japanese papers. I was fortunate enough to have a friend who brought me a sheaf of exquisite paper back from Japan, but the paper is available at most good craft suppliers. I used some of the paper to make several of the projects in this book.

In this volume I have covered all of the popular papercrafting techniques to make a wide variety of items. I hope you enjoy constructing the projects, trying out new techniques and using the ideas as inspiration for your own creativity. All of the techniques used are described in detail on pages 14–27, once you've mastered them you will find the possibilities for making great items are endless. The galleries (see pages 146–149) are packed with even more new and different designs.

Happy papercrafting!

▲ **Halloween brings plenty of opportunities to practise your paper crafting. This card has been created using peel-offs, punched leaves and cut-out bats.**

1/Materials and Techniques

WHETHER YOU ARE NEW TO PAPERCRAFTING OR AN OLD HAND, YOU WILL FIND THERE ARE ALWAYS INTERESTING AND INVENTIVE TOOLS AND MATERIALS TO CONSIDER AND NEW TECHNIQUES TO TRY. I HAVE COLLECTED A WONDERFUL SELECTION OF PAPERS, PAINTS AND OTHER CRAFT MATERIALS OVER THE YEARS. I FIND THAT A GOOD STORAGE SYSTEM FOR MY EQUIPMENT AND PAPERS IS ESSENTIAL. I KEEP MY TOOLS IN LARGE TRAYS AND THE PAPER IS NEATLY FILED AWAY TO ENSURE THAT SHEETS REMAIN IN PRISTINE CONDITION UNTIL THEY ARE REQUIRED.

Materials

PAPER

From the finest tissue paper to the thickest card, paper and card are available in almost any shade, weight, quality and texture. Almost all paper is machine-made, although most craft shops carry stocks of paper that is made, coloured and decorated by hand. A wide selection of paper and card is available through most good stationery and craft stores and online. There is a standard grading and measurement system for paper: paper is graded by weight and measured in a system from A1 to A10. Occasionally I buy paper in large sheets, but most of my paper is purchased ready-cut to A5 (148 x 210 mm/5¾ x 8¼ in) and A4 (210 x 297 mm/8¼ x 11¾ in). Sheets of

paper in these sizes are easy to store and they are less likely to be damaged in transit. Paper cut to A4 is the most widely available at retail outlets.

Store your paper flat if possible. I find filing shelves very useful and have two stacks: one for pristine sheets of paper and card and another for cut paper and card. By filing left-over paper away according to colour I can quickly see that little piece needed from which to punch a flower or to complete a small project. If it is impractical to store large sheets of

▼ **Just a small selection from my collection of paper: a mixture of gift-wrap, handmade paper, card and beautiful washi paper from Japan.**

paper flat, roll and store upright in a container. If crumpled, handmade and tissue paper can often be ironed smooth at a low temperature and restored to glory. Once card or machine-made paper is folded or crushed, however, it is almost impossible to restore.

When working with paper and card consider the project before you decide what weight and texture of paper to use. Lay out your chosen paper and card together on the work surface before you begin to ensure that the colours and textures work well together. Finding the right shade of, say, pink or blue can make all the difference to giving a project a professional finish.

EQUIPMENT FOR CUTTING AND SCORING

Cutting mat (1)
A cutting mat is an essential item.

Craft knives (2)
A good, sharp craft knife is essential for cutting neat edges. Always use a craft knife in conjunction with a metal ruler. Cut against the ruler and always work on a cutting mat. Keep knives and blades out of the reach of children.

Rulers (3)
You will need a steel ruler to cut against and clear ruler to aid measuring. A set square is also very useful.

Embossing tool (4)
Use this tool to score paper and card. A scored line is easy to fold and once smoothed down gives a crisper, neater finish.

Scissors (5)

I consider good scissors an investment and always buy the best scissors I can afford. Take good care of them. Non-stick scissors are invaluable; I have a large pair and a small pair. Once you have used non-stick scissors you will be converted.

Paper trimmer (7)

Not a necessity, but a paper trimmer is very useful if you are cutting up large sheets of paper and card into smaller pieces.

Decorative scissors (8)

A whole array of different decorative scissors are available. Some are for decorating the paper's edge, others for corners.

Shape cutters

I find commercial shape cutters extremely useful and wouldn't be without them. They make cutting out shaped windows and frames so simple and are available in circles, ovals, squares and numerous other shapes. Always use them according to the manufacturer's instructions and practise on scrap paper and card to perfect your technique.

ADHESIVES

Glitter glue (9)

I love glitter and use it often, but it is nearly impossible to totally eliminate any glitter spills. Glitter glue is a less messy option, easier to clean up after and you never get dry glitter spills.

PVA (craft) glue (10)

PVA glue is white glue suitable for use on paper and card. It dries clear and can be thinned with water. To apply PVA glue you could pour a little glue into a container and use an applicator of some sort, such as a brush, or even a cocktail stick, depending on the job at hand. I have recycled a small squeezy container with a nozzle and use that to apply glue. I find this method works well – with practice you can control the quantities of glue coming through the nozzle and will avoid wastage. Occasionally the nozzle will gum up but this is easily solved by pushing a straight pin through it to release the blockage.

Glue stick (11)

A useful alternative to PVA adhesive, and very useful when attaching sheets of paper to one another. Remember to replace the lid after use as glue sticks have a tendency to dry out.

1. Cutting mat
2. Craft knife
3. Rulers
4. Embossing tool
5. Scissors
6. Pencil
7. Paper trimmer
8. Decorative scissors
9. Glitter glue
10. PVA (craft) glue
11. Glue stick
12. Adhesive photo corners
13. 3D sticky foam pads
14. Adhesive tape
15. Double-sided adhesive tape

Adhesive photo corners (12)

These are useful when mounting photographs in a scrapbook or photo album. Particularly good if you don't actually want to put anything sticky on the photo.

3D sticky foam pads (13)

This is double-sided tape laid over a spongy foam. Using these pads raises the taped item off the page. Brilliant for decoupage and pop-ups.

Adhesive tape (14)

Adhesive tape comes in a variety of widths, colours and strengths. I like to keep a low-tack adhesive tape handy along with a tape that sticks clear.

Double-sided adhesive tape (15)

(see photo top right on page 11) Double-sided adhesive tape is easy to use, clean and practically invisible. It comes in a variety of widths and dispensers. I often use double-sided tape instead of glue for a clean finish.

Aerosol glue

Aerosol glue gives a quick clean finish and is very useful when sticking thin papers, such as mulberry paper or tissue paper, and in decoupage. Always follow the manufacturer's instructions for the specific type of glue that you purchase.

Silicone gel

A clear gel available in tube dispensers. The glue is thick and fairly solid. You squeeze a little on, and it will stick two objects together while creating a 3D effect.

DECORATIVE MATERIALS

Felt-tip pens (1)

A set of felt-tips play a useful role in papercrafting. There are different types of felt-tips, so use the right pen for the job. Store your felt-tips with the caps firmly on.

Gel pens (2)

These are highly versatile pens that are lovely to decorate items with. The quality of the ink is very good and the colours are amazing. They are effective on light and dark papers.

Coloured pencils (3)

Good sharp pencils are essential when marking up projects, and coloured pencils are great for decoration.

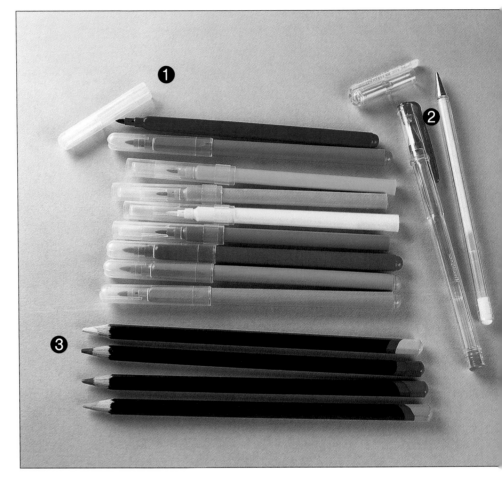

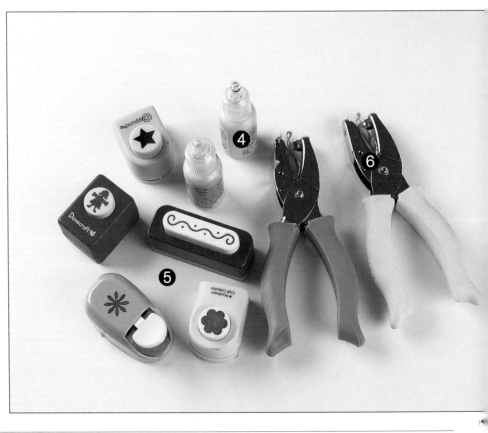

1. **Felt-tip pens**
2. **Gel pens**
3. **Coloured pencils**
4. **3D paint**
5. **Punches**
6. **Scissor punches**
7. **Rainbow ink pad**
8. **Precision heat tool**
9. **Rubber stamps**
10. **Embossing powders**
11. **Embossing pen**
12. **Embossing pad**
13. **Ink pads**

Paints (4)

3D paint is great for highlighting and creating patterns. I have a small box of watercolours, which I find very useful.

Punches (5/6)

Punches cut shapes from paper and thin card. Use punched shapes to create your own motifs and decorate craft projects. Punches in basic shapes – such as discs, squares, leaves, etc. – are very useful.

Ink pads (7/13)

Stamped images can be printed using ink pads in almost any colour, or by loading the stamp with ink from a felt-tip pen.

Precision heat tool (8)

A precision heat tool is necessary to seal embossing powder. This tool should be used with care and you must always use according to the manufacturer's instructions. Keep your hands and the paper that is being heated a safe distance from the heat source.

Cut-outs, peel-offs and stickers

Cut-outs, stickers and peel-offs play a useful role in papercrafts. They are an instant way to add colour and decoration, meaning that they are a quick and stylish option.

Rubber stamps (9)

Rubber stamps are available in a huge variety of designs. Stamped images can be used on their own, in mixed-medium projects or cut out and used in decoupage.

Embossing powders (10)

Come in a wide variety of colours and are used in conjunction with an embossing pad.

Embossing pen (11)

Use an embossing pen along with embossing powder for freehand embossing. Do not use regular felt-tip pens as their ink dries too quickly.

Embossing pads (12)

This is a pad of slow-drying liquid, which, once stamped on paper, can be sprinkled with embossing powder and then sealed with a precision heat tool (see page 22).

Techniques

SCORING, FOLDING, TEARING AND CUTTING

Measuring up

Before cutting, you will need to measure up. Use a clean ruler and make light pencil lines, as these will generally need to be erased once you have cut your paper or card.

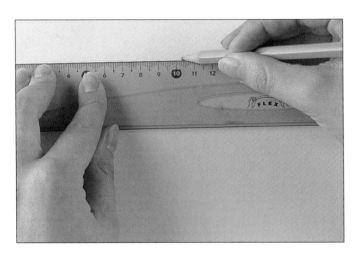

Cutting with a craft knife and metal ruler

When cutting give yourself plenty of room. Ensure your craft knife has a sharp blade and the ruler is clean. ALWAYS cut against a metal ruler. Not only does this ensure good clean lines but you are also less likely to cut yourself.

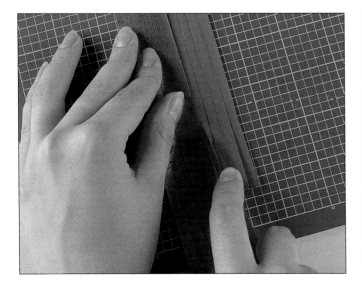

Tearing against a ruler

Measure and mark up the line to be torn. Fold and then tear against a ruler.

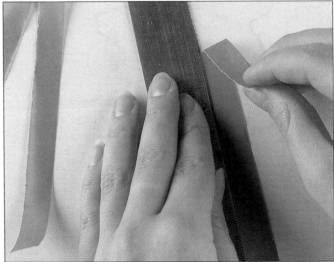

Tearing with the grain

Like wood, paper has a grain, which means that it will tear in a straight line one way but not another. Take a sheet of paper and tear it first one way and then the other. This will demonstrate the ease with which you can tear a straight line with the grain and just how difficult it is to do this against the grain.

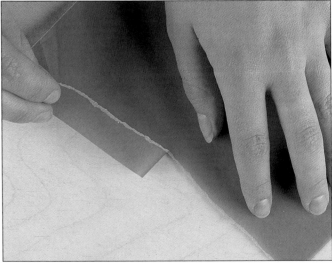

Tearing against the grain

When you tear against the grain the tear line will be uneven and uncontrollable. But sometimes this may be the effect that you're looking for.

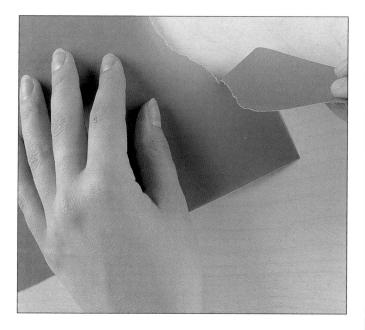

Scoring

Use a pencil and ruler to mark the line that you want to score. Next, lay a ruler along the marked-up line. Take your embossing tool and run it firmly down the paper along the ruler's edge. Fold the paper along the scored line. Finally use a bone folder (or you can use something like the back of a spoon) to really give the fold a crisp finish.

Folding valley folds

A valley fold is scored on the underside of the paper or card so the fold points away from you. Use a bone folder to ensure the fold is sharp.

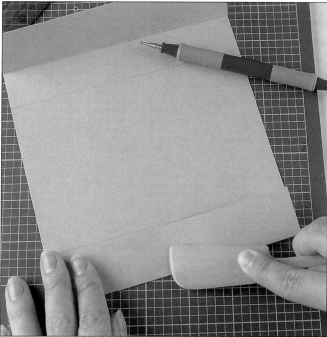

Folding hill folds

A hill fold is scored on the front of the card or paper and folded so the fold points towards you.

Folding into the centre line

First measure the width of the paper. Halve this to give you the centre. Use a ruler and pencil to mark this point with a dot at the top and bottom edges of the paper.

① Rule a light pencil line down the centre using the dots as a guide.

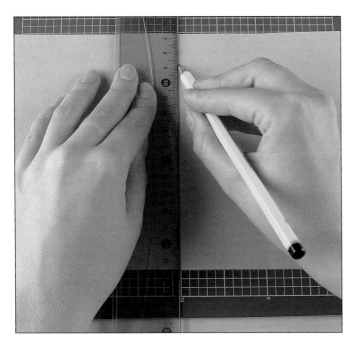

② Fold one vertical edge of the paper inwards to the centre line and use your bone folder to give the fold a crisp edge.

 Repeat with the other edge of the paper.

MAKING A BOX

You can buy blank boxes from craft shops or recycle a used box by covering it with paper. If you would like to construct a box you could do it in any number of ways, but here I demonstrate a really simple way. If you want to make a box of a different size to the one shown here, practise first by making this box then simply create a template to the size that you want.

① Use the diagrams on page 152 (Daisy boxes) to draw out the base and lid. Cut out around the outer line.

② Score along the dotted lines and cut along the solid lines.

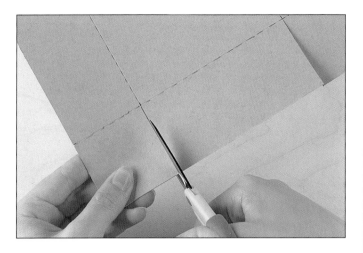

③ Fold into shape. Use PVA (craft) glue or double-sided adhesive tape to hold the box in shape.

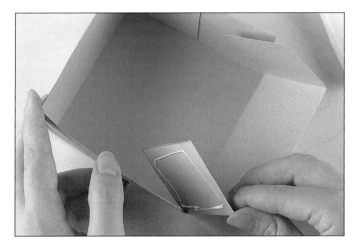

④ The base of the box is slightly smaller than the lid.

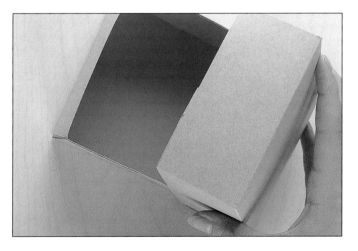

MAKING A BAG

This way of making a bag is so simple. You basically 'wrap' the paper around an object to get the basic 'body' of the bag. Here I have used a book. You will need the same size piece of paper as if you were going to gift-wrap the book.

① Make a shallow fold at the bottom of the sheet of paper. Place the paper, fold side up on your work surface.

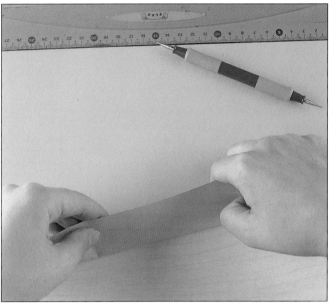

② Place the book centrally on the paper and fold up the paper around the book. Make sure the overlap is reasonably central, then glue the overlap.

③ Use your fingertips to sharpen up the four vertical folds.

④ Fold in the edges at the bottom of the bag as if you were wrapping a parcel. Fold down the upper and lower flaps and glue firmly in place.

⑤ Once the glue has set remove the book. Make a handle from a strip of paper and glue to the inside edges of the bag.

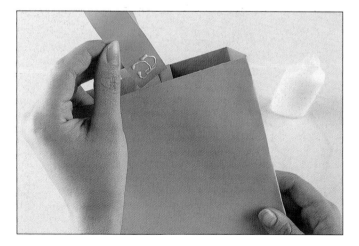

MAKING AN ENVELOPE

Envelopes are available in a wide range of sizes and colours. You can embellish ready-made ones with rubber stamps, punches, stickers, transfers, basically anything you like. Envelopes are simple to make, as shown here.

① Trace the template on page 151. Cut around the outside line, score and fold into shape.

② Apply glue on the marked areas. For the top flap, either tuck it inside, or a special envelope glue is available that once applied to the envelope flap will dry and can be moistened later to seal the envelope.

③ If you are going to the trouble of making an envelope you might as well decorate it with a special embellishment, here are a couple of suggestions. You could decorate the inner part of the envelope with punched-out shapes...

④ ...or cut a piece of paper that will fit inside the envelope. Punch shapes in the paper insert and then glue in place.

A SIMPLE POP-UP

Pop-ups are not difficult to make. As with most things, the secret is practice. When creating pop-ups the trick is neat, straight cuts exactly in place, precise scoring and sharp folds. Here I demonstrate how to create a simple pop-up motif card.

① Fold a sheet of A5 (148 x 210 mm/5¾ x 8¼ in) paper in half to create the card blank. Mark the vertical centre of the card. Cut a strip of thin card, 1 cm (½ in) wide and 8 cm (3 in) in length. Mark the horizontal centre of the strip and score a line. Measure in 1 cm (½ in) from each end and

score a line. Fold the scored lines – they are all hill folds – so the crease of the fold points towards you.

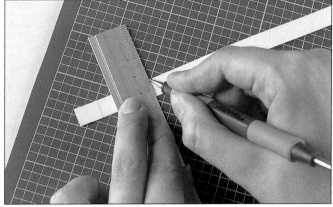

② Apply glue to the 1 cm (½ in) flaps that you have created at each end of the strip. Place the strip across the centre of the card, ensuring that the central fold of the strip sits exactly on the centre of the card.

③ Glue a simple motif to the strip. Allow the glue to dry. Open up the card and the image should pop up!

USING PUNCHES

Punches are amongst the most useful of paper tools. They come in a wide variety of shapes, sizes and motifs. In fact, it's almost possible to find a punch of absolutely anything you can think of.

Positioning punches

To ensure the punched shape is cut in the correct spot, turn the punch over and insert the paper to the point required.

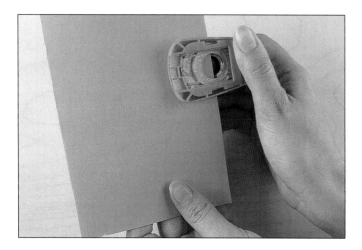

Punched edges

Edging punches are useful when creating a layered effect. Here the edging punch has been used on the cover of a greetings card, with a darker-coloured card placed beneath to highlight the punched-out shapes.

Using a punch to create a motif

This is an example of how using one punch and different coloured papers, you can create a motif with a little more detail than the basic punched shape. Take a wine glass punch. Punch the shape out of clear cellophane and from yellow card. Trim the yellow wine glass – cut off a small strip across the top of the glass, and cut off the stem and base. Glue this shape beneath the clear, cellophane wine glass. You now have a glass of white wine. An example of using a shoe punch in a similar way is also shown in the picture.

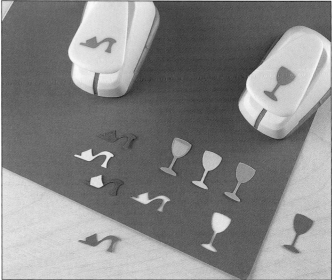

Punches that make completed items

Some punches are quite sophisticated – for example this stamp cuts and scores a mini envelope. All you have to do is fold and stick!

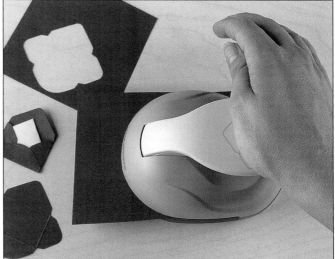

HOW TO USE TRANSFERS

Transfers are designs that are printed on a sheet of acetate. To transfer the design from the acetate to paper, position the transfer and then rub over it firmly with an embossing tool or something like a lolly stick would also do the same job. Make sure you rub over the whole of the design.

USING PEEL-OFFS

Peel-offs have the same immediacy as stickers, but with a little input from the crafter they can be made even more effective. You can embellish the basic shape by sticking it on coloured card and cutting it out, or colouring it in with paint, pencils or inks.

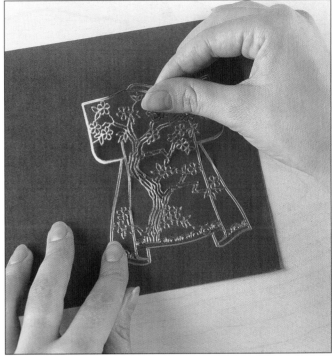

USING STICKERS

Stickers can be very useful when papercrafting as they are so quick to use and there are literally thousands of designs to choose from.

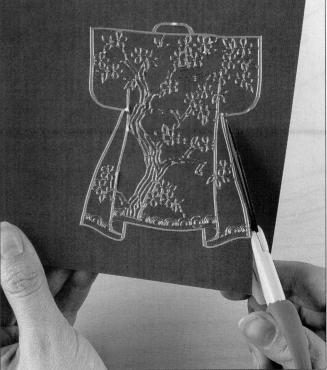

USING RUBBER STAMPS

Rubber stamping is a technique whereby patterns, letters and pictures are printed using a rubber stamp and inked stamp pad.

Stamping on to paper

Press the stamp on to the ink pad, then press firmly on to the paper. Lift the stamp straight off the paper and set aside the stamped motif to allow it to dry.

Stamping an embossed design

① Press the stamp on to an embossing pad. Press the stamp on to the paper.

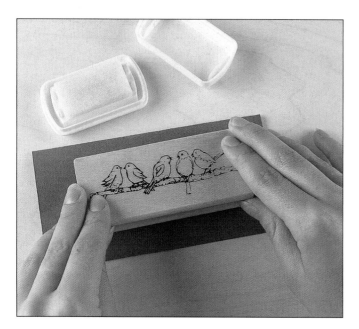

② Sprinkle the stamped image with embossing powder. This is best done over a sheet of scrap paper so as to catch any spills. Shake off any excess powder from the stamped design on to the scrap paper and return it to the container.

③ Use a precision heat tool to seal the powder. You must follow the manufacturer's instructions.

WEAVING

Weaving is an ancient craft, which can be as simple or as complicated as you'd like to make it. In papercraft, weaving can be used to represent an object, for example a basket, or as a decoration in its own right, or embellished with a shaped or plain frame on a card.

1 Cut equally spaced vertical slits into your piece of card, stopping before you get to the other edge. This creates a fringed effect.

2 Cut lengths of paper, roughly the same width as the fringed strips. Insert the first length into the fringing, so that it goes under the first strip, over the second strip etc. When you insert your next length, it should go over the first strip, under the second etc.

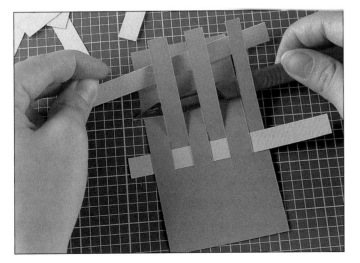

3 Continue in this way, alternating between weaving over and weaving under.

WINDOWS AND APERTURES

The easiest way to cut windows and apertures is with a commercial cutting tool. If you don't have one of these, you can of course do it by hand, but you need to work carefully and slowly to ensure that your shape is accurate.

1 Choose the image that you want to place within a window. Position it under the various shapes to see what will suit it best.

2 Place your piece of card that is going to have the window cut out of it under the template. Use the cutting tool to cut out the window.

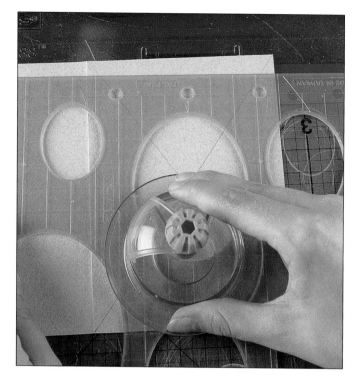

3 Stick your chosen image behind the window.

LACE PAPER CUTTING

Repeat geometric cutting patterns are folded to produce colourful and decorative patterns. Templates are available to buy.

1 Place the template on top of the card. Use a pencil to mark the pattern on the card.

2 Tape the card to a cutting mat and, using a craft knife, carefully cut the lines.

③ Fold the paper back.

④ Stick the finished design onto a piece of contrasting coloured card to display the pattern.

QUILLING

This is the art of rolling thin strips of paper into different shapes and using the shapes to form designs. A quilling tool, along with paper strips can be purchased from most craft outlets.

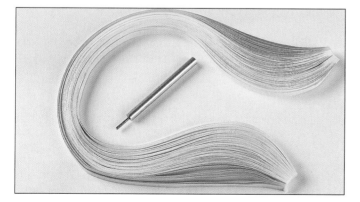

① Thread the paper strip through the narrow loop at the end of the quilling tool.

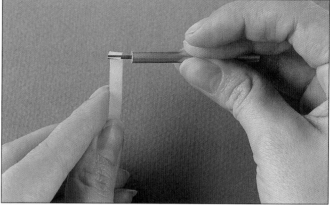

② Wind the paper around the tool. When a coil of sufficient size has been created, remove the tool.

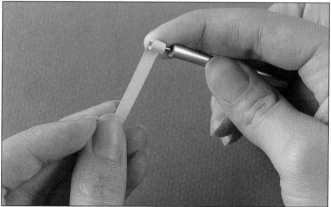

③ The coil can then be shaped.

◄ **A quilling tool and paper strips.**

MAKING FLOWERS

Flowers are one of the most popular motifs. Here is a selection.

1 Stamp three daisy images and emboss in white on blue paper. Cut the images out and layer up with glue. Dot white 3D paint in the centre of the flower.

2 Punch daisy images from thin coloured card and embellish with 3D paint.

3 Punch small flowers from thin blue card and embellish with yellow 3D paint to make forget-me-nots.

4 Punch medium flowers from thin card and cut to separate the petals. Lift the petals up slightly and layer one on top of another. Embellish the centre with a 3D paint dot.

5 Punch medium flowers out of violet paper and decorate with 3D paint.

6 Stamp a flower image and emboss with black embossing powder. Embellish with red 3D paint.

7 16 Cut flowers from sheets of decorative gift-wrap.

8 A flower sticker.

9 Punch medium flowers from thin white card and cut to separate the petals. Quill a strip of white paper for the centre of the flowers.

10 A flower formed from 3D paint dots.

11 Decorate a punched flowerpot and green leaves with flower stickers to create this pretty pot plant.

12 Lay heart- and leaf-shaped gems on to narrow strips of card to create these romantic flowers.

13 Quilled and fringe a strip of yellow paper, tightly roll then push a a spotted paper fastener through the centre.

14 Punch out daffodils, first from green paper then from yellow. Cut out the yellow blossoms and glue on top of the green blossoms.

15 Punch and layer flowers, and embellish with 3D paint.

17 Punch a heart shape and embellish with a punched daisy.

18 A sticker.

19 Form a pretty flower from quilled strips of purple and yellow paper.

20 Punch daisy shapes from opaque pink paper.

21 Stamp and emboss a daisy in red, and give it a white centre.

22 Cut a pretty daisy from a paper table napkin.

23 Emboss and colour a stamped image.

24 Punch a large flower and raise the petal edges. Embellish the flower with purple 3D paint.

25 Pink and purple flower-shaped paper fasteners.

26 Punch flowers from yellow and pink gingham paper and layer. Embellish the flowers with pink 3D paint.

2/Boxes

BOXES CAN BE SIMPLY FASHIONED FROM CARD OR PAPER, FOLDED ORIGAMI-STYLE OR FORMED FROM A CUT-OUT SHAPE. WHAT FOLLOWS IS A SIMPLE SELECTION OF BOXES MADE, DECORATED AND EMBELLISHED USING A VARIETY OF TECHNIQUES AND MATERIALS. ONCE YOU HAVE MASTERED A FEW OF THE CONSTRUCTION METHODS YOU CAN HAVE FUN CREATING YOUR OWN CO-ORDINATED PACKAGING FOR GIFTS AND FOR STORING ITEMS IN THE HOME.

Keepsake box

I found this sheet of gift-wrap, decorated with images of flowers, pots and baskets, some time ago and I knew it was destined for a special project. The sage green paper covering the box certainly enhances the delicate flowers and basket. If you can't find a similar sheet of gift-wrap you could use stickers instead. Stick them on to a sheet of paper first and then cut them out in the same way as you would cut out the images from the gift-wrap.

YOU WILL NEED

A3 (297 x 420 mm/
   11¾ x 23½ in) sheet
   white card
Scissors
PVA (craft) glue
A3 (297 x 420 mm/
   11¾ x 23½ in) sheet
   green card
Suitable gift-wrap
Glue stick
A5 (148 x 210 mm/
   5¾ x 8¼ in) sheet thin
   white card
Double-sided adhesive
   tape
3D sticky foam pads

1 Using the diagram on page 150 draw the box base and lid on to the white card. Cut out the base and lid. Score and fold. Use PVA glue to stick in place. Cover the box and lid neatly with green card.

2 Now make the inner shell of the base and lid. For the base measure up a piece of white card 8.5 x 12.5 cm (3½ x 4¾ in). Cover this with gift-wrap and use PVA glue to stick in place on the base of the box. Next cut out the side pieces, you will need two measuring 8.5 x 5.5 cm (3½ x 2¼ in) and two measuring 12.5 x 5.5 cm (43/4 x 2¼ in). Cover them with gift-wrap and glue in place. For the lid cut one piece of white card 12.5 x 8.5 cm (4¾ x 3½ in), cover with gift-wrap and stick in place. Cut two pieces 12 x 1 cm (4½ x ½ in) and two pieces 8.5 x 1cm (3½ x ½ in), cover and stick in place. Now your box is ready to embellish.

3 Choose the main image that is going to decorate the box lid. You will need two cut-outs of this image. Choose a couple of other smaller images that complement the main image – you will only need one of each of these images. Using a glue stick, attach the images to a piece of thin white card. Use scissors to carefully cut out the images.

4 Cut a piece of white card 9 x 6.5 cm (3½ x 2¾ in). Use double-sided tape to attach it to the lid of the box in a central position. Cut a piece of green card 5 x 8 cm (2 x 3¼ in) and attach this centrally on the white card. Cut a piece of white card 7.5 x 4.5 cm (3 x 1¾ in) and attach this centrally on the green card. Stick the small images in place using PVA glue, then position the first cut-out of the main image. Place a few 3D sticky foam pads on to the main image then position the second cut-out directly on top of the first.

Baby memory box

Embellished borders are very much *en vogue* and can bring something special to a project. I have created my own border for this box which could become the special place to store mementoes of a baby's first few weeks: keep safe the tiny first slippers, greetings cards and photographs. This memory box is as useful as it is attractive.

YOU WILL NEED

Box suitable for
  covering (a shoe box
  is ideal)
Pink gingham gift-wrap
Glue stick
A4 (210 x 297 mm/
  8¼ x 11¾ in) sheet thin
  white card
Craft knife
Cutting mat
Metal ruler
Embossing pad
Teddy bear rubber
  stamp
White embossing
  powder
Scrap paper
Precision heat tool
  (see page 13)
Scissors
Punches: large,
  medium, small flower,
  small daisy, disc
2 sheets A4 (210 x
  297 mm/8¼ x 11¾ in)
  paper each in: pastel
  green, pink, yellow,
  white
PVA (craft) glue
3D sticky foam pads
3D paint in yellow, pink,
  blue
Double-sided adhesive
  tape

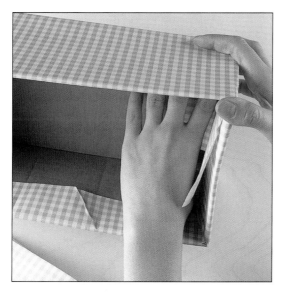

TIP

YOU COULD ALSO CREATE A BORDER USING STAMPED IMAGES, STICKERS OR PEEL-OFFS. WHEN DESIGNING YOUR OWN BORDER BEGIN BY CHOOSING A STYLE, THEN A COLOUR SCHEME. BEAR IN MIND YOU WILL NEED IMAGES IN A VARIETY OF SIZES TO GIVE VISUAL INTEREST AND ALLOW YOU TO LAYER AND FILL IN GAPS. CHOOSE A FEW FEATURE IMAGES AND PLENTY OF SMALLER ONES.

---

1 Begin by covering the box, inside and out, with pink gingham paper.

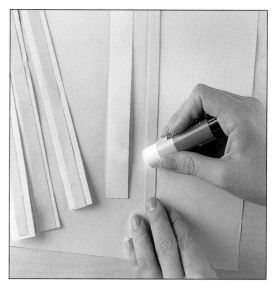

2 Cut strips of thin white card 2 cm (¾ in) wide and the length of the A4 sheet. Cut strips of the pink paper 1 cm (½ in) wide and 30 cm (11 in) long. Use a glue stick to attach the pink paper strips centrally on the white card strips.

③ Using the embossing pad and the teddy bear stamp, stamp images on to the green paper. You will need seven teddy bears in all. Sprinkle with embossing powder, shake off the excess and seal with the precision heat tool. Cut out the teddy bears, leaving a narrow border around the embossed images. Punch out plenty of flowers, daisies and discs using the coloured papers and the gingham gift-wrap.

④ Use PVA glue to attach smaller flowers in the centre of large ones, place flowers on discs and discs in the centre of flowers. Use PVA glue to attach six of the teddy bears and some of the flowers randomly along the prepared white and pink strips. When the strips are about two thirds covered, attach some flowers with 3D sticky foam pads. Review your design every now and then. You need to really smother the strips with flowers.

⑤ When you are happy with your design and the glue has dried, embellish the strips with 3D paint. When dry, attach to the edges of the lid of the box, using double-sided tape. Cut three rectangles: one from pink card – 15.5 x 6 cm (6 x 2¼ in); one from green card – 15 x 5 cm (6 x 2 in); one from white card – 14.5 x 4.5 cm (5¾ x 1¾ in). Layer up, white on green on pink. Embellish it with a teddy bear, a few flowers and 3D paint. When dry, attach it centrally on one of the long sides of the box. You can write the baby's name on this label.

Origami boxes

Paper folding is a useful skill. This box is not difficult to make and once you have mastered the art you can make the box to fit the gift! If you use paper, a double thickness is good and if you use card it will need to be thin card to enable the folds to be crisp and smooth.

YOU WILL NEED

A4 (210 x 297 mm/
  8¼ x 11¾ in) sheet thin
  yellow card

Cutting mat

Craft knife

Ruler

Pencil

Bone folder

Scraps of red and
  green paper

PVA (craft) glue

Large flower punch

Leaf punch

Yellow 3D paint

1 Cut the yellow card in half. Set aside one sheet. Cut 7 mm (⅜ in) from the length and 7 mm (⅜ in) from the width of the sheet. Position the sheet with the longest side towards you. Measure the length of the paper and mark the centre point. Rule a light pencil line horizontally across the paper from this point.

2 Fold each side of the sheet in to the central pencil line. Make a crisp fold by using your bone folder.

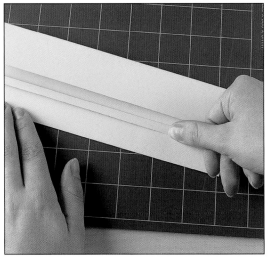

3 Fold back a strip approximately 8 mm (¼ in) wide on each flap. Ensure this fold is crisp and flat.

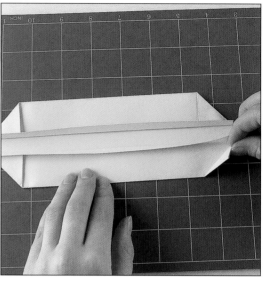

④ Fold the corners inward to the fold line, tucking them under the 8-mm (¼-in) backward fold.

▲ **It is important that the colours work well together and here red, yellow and green make for a bright, fresh combination. Try making another box using other colours to get a totally different effect.**

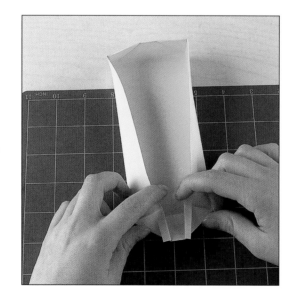

⑤ Place your fingers into the corners and lift the box into shape. Repeat steps 1–5 with the second piece of yellow card (except do not trim anything off this piece). You now have two boxes, one slightly larger than the other. The larger box is the lid. Decorate the box lid. Cut strips of red paper and stick them on to the box to create the impression of a ribbon.

⑥ Punch three leaves out of green paper. To create the veins fold each leaf in half lengthways and in half on the diagonal. Open out. Punch six flowers out of red paper. Glue two flowers together. Repeat for the other flowers, so that you have three double flowers in total. Cut in between a couple of the petals and 'pinch' the flower together so that it is raised. Glue the flowers and leaves on the lid. Use 3D paint to embellish the flowers.

Daisy boxes

I found this daisy punch and couldn't resist it. The daisy shape lends itself well to paper architecture when layered up, and when flat makes a great image cut out of tissue paper or patterned paper. It is also effective when used to decorate a plain sheet of paper to be used as gift-wrap. The box is simply cut and folded from blue card and the interior decorated with stamped white daisies, continuing the daisy theme.

YOU WILL NEED

2 A4 (210 x 297 mm/
 8¼ x 11¾ in) sheets
 violet card
Craft knife
Cutting mat
Metal ruler
Embossing tool
Daisy rubber stamp
Embossing pad
Scrap paper
White embossing
 powder
Precision heat tool
 (see page 13)
Double-sided adhesive
 tape
A4 (210 x 297 mm/
 8¼ x 11¾ in) sheet thin
 white card
A5 (148 x 210 mm/
 5¾ x 8¼ in) sheet
 yellow textured card
Large daisy punch
Circle cutter
Pencil
PVA (craft) glue

1 Use the diagrams on page 152 to draw the base and lid on the violet card. Cut out the base and lid. Score and cut as marked. Use the daisy stamp to emboss the inside of the lid and base. Sprinkle the stamped daisies with white embossing powder, shake off the excess and seal with the precision heat tool.

2 Fold the base and lid into shape, and hold in place with double-sided tape.

TIP

IN THE PHOTO ON PAGE 40, AN ALTERNATIVE BOX DESIGN IS SHOWN ON THE LEFT. ONCE YOU'VE PERFECTED YOUR BOX CONSTRUCTION SKILLS, TRY MAKING THIS DIFFERENT, TALLER BOX. THIS TIME DECORATE THE EXTERIOR OF THE BASE AND LID WITH THE STAMPED DAISY DESIGN AND MAKE THE TOP DECORATION IN EXACTLY THE SAME WAY AS YOU DID FOR THE MAIN PROJECT. YOU COULD ALSO TRY MAKING A LONG, HORIZONTAL BOX AND DECORATE IT WITH THREE DAISIES.

3 To construct the flower you need three daisy shapes cut from thin white card (either use the daisy punch or use the template on page 152), and one circle, 2 cm (¾ in) in diameter, cut from textured yellow card.

4 Stack the three daisies one on top of the other. Curl each petal over a pencil, gently smoothing it so each petal has a nice curve.

5 Separate the daisies and use PVA glue to attach them one on top of the other, overlapping the petals. Stick the yellow circle in the centre of the daisy. Attach the completed daisy to the lid of the box.

Little cut and fold box

This little box can hold party favours or wedding confetti, or a small gift such as earrings or a special brooch. Made out of paper, it is easy to make and holds its shape well. In addition to the main project, the image opposite shows a couple of alternatives made using gift-wrap and wallpaper off-cuts.

YOU WILL NEED
2 A4 (210 x 297 mm/
   8¼ x 11¾ in) sheets
   violet paper
Pencil
Craft knife
Cutting mat
Metal ruler
Embossing tool
PVA (craft) glue
Scraps of coloured
   papers
Butterfly punch
Tweezers

1 Use the templates on page 153 to cut the base and lid out of the violet paper. Cut two 6 cm (2¼ in) squares of violet paper to line the base and lid.

2 Fold the base and lid into shape. Use PVA glue to glue the lining of the lid and base in place. Cut two strips of paper 1 cm (½ in) wide and 30 cm (12 in) long. Attach to the box lid, forming a cross, using PVA glue. Fold the excess under the rim.

3 Punch six butterflies out of the scraps of paper. Stick the butterflies in place, so that you have three, two-layer butterflies. As the butterflies are quite small, use tweezers to help you place them.

3 /Cards

A HANDMADE CARD IS BOTH A GREETING AND A GIFT, OFTEN MADE WITH THE RECIPIENT IN MIND, AND THE POSSIBILITIES FOR EMBELLISHMENT ARE ALMOST ENDLESS. I HAVE INCLUDED SOME DESIGNS THAT ARE VERY QUICK AND EASY TO MAKE SO THAT THEY CAN BE MASS PRODUCED, BUT THERE ARE ALSO SOME PROJECTS FOR YOU TO TAKE YOUR TIME OVER. DESIGNS FOR INVITATIONS ARE ALSO INCLUDED IN THIS CHAPTER.

Christmas stamps

Christmas means lots of greetings cards, and this simple yet appealing card has been designed with mass production in mind. I used a stamp punch and some seasonal stickers to create the impression of Christmas stamps. You may want to create a similar effect using real stamps saved from received mail.

YOU WILL NEED

Mottled grey card,
    10.5 x 21 cm
    (4¼ x 8½ in)
Ruler
Embossing tool
Stamp punch
A5 (148 x 210 mm/
    5¾ x 8¼ in) sheet white
    card
A5 (148 x 210 mm/
    5¾ x 8¼ in) sheet blue
    card
Scissors
Glue stick
Seasonal stickers
Red card, 5 x 5 cm
    (2 x 2 in)
Double-sided adhesive
    tape
3D sticky foam pads
Silver 3D paint

1 Fold the mottled grey card in half to create the card blank. Using the stamp punch, cut out one white and one blue stamp shape. Cut carefully around the blue stamped shape removing the serrated edge.

2 Glue the blue card centrally on to the white stamp. Choose a suitable sticker and attach it centrally on the blue card.

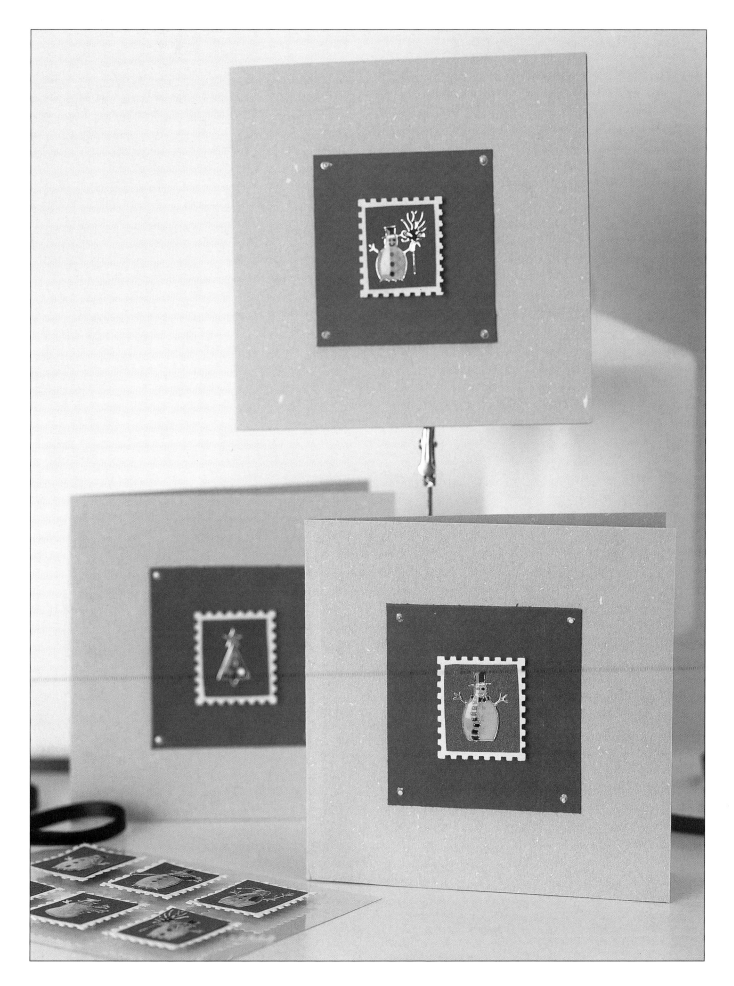

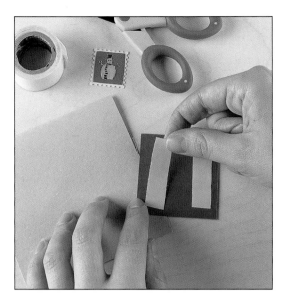

③ Attach double-sided tape to the piece of red card and place centrally on the front of the card blank.

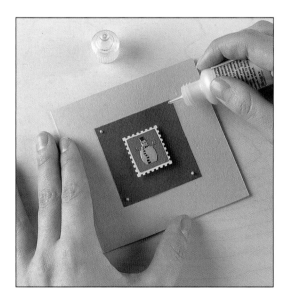

④ Place a couple of 3D sticky foam pads on the reverse of the central stamp motif and stick in the centre of the red card. Embellish the red card with a 3D silver paint dot, one in each corner.

TIP

AS THIS CARD IS SO QUICK AND EASY TO MAKE, YOU'VE GOT NO EXCUSE NOT TO MAKE ALL YOUR OWN CHRISTMAS CARDS. IF YOU'RE GOING TO MAKE LOTS, GET ALL OF THE INDIVIDUAL ELEMENTS READY FIRST. CUT AND FOLD THE CARD BASES, ASSEMBLE THE CENTRAL STAMP MOTIF, PLACE DOUBLE-SIDED ADHESIVE TAPE ON THE BACK OF THE RED CARD. THIS WAY YOU HAVE EVERYTHING TO HAND AND YOU CAN MAKE A FEW CARDS EACH DAY IN THE RUN-UP TO CHRISTMAS. IF YOU DON'T HAVE TIME TO MAKE ENVELOPES, BUY THEM, AND PUT A STICKER ON THE FLAP.

▲ **This close-up photo of the card decoration shows the detail in the sticker – certainly Christmas cute! If you can't find these stickers, just use something similar.**

Sunshine flowers

This card is made using the iris folding technique. This technique got its name because the spiral effect that is produced resembles the iris of an eye or camera.

YOU WILL NEED

A5 (148 x 210 mm/ 5¾ x 8¼ in) sheet blue card
Pencil
Ruler
Oval cutter, 10.5 x 8 cm (4 x 3 in)
Low-tack adhesive tape
A4 (210 x 297 mm/ 8¼ x 11¾ in) sheets yellow in three shades
Paper trimmer
Adhesive tape
Scissors
A5 (148 x 210 mm/ 5¾ x 8¼ in) sheet white card
Double-sided tape
PVA (craft) glue
Daisy punch
3D paint yellow

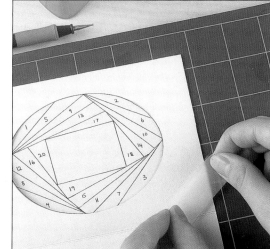

1 Fold the blue card in half to form the card blank. Open up the card. On the reverse of the front of the card draw diagonal lines from corner to corner to find the centre. Use the oval cutter to cut out an oval window in the centre of the front of the card. Photocopy or trace the folding pattern on page 152. Lay the folding pattern under the oval window (with the inside of the card facing you). Use low-tack tape to keep the card and pattern in place.

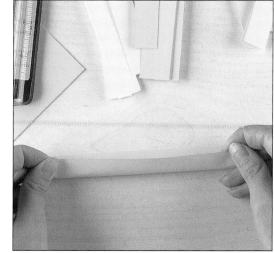

2 Prepare the yellow paper strips. Each strip should measure 4 x 10 cm (1½ x 4 in). You will need eight pale yellow strips, eight medium yellow strips and four dark yellow strips. Fold each strip in half lengthways.

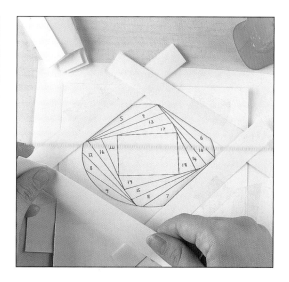

3 Following the numbered pattern put the paper strips in place. Start with the palest yellow strips and attach the first strip over area 1, the second over area 2 etc. Continue with the medium yellow strips and then the dark yellow strips. Where the strips cross, stick them down with adhesive tape.

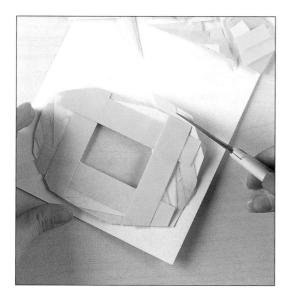

④ Once the strips are all in place, remove the pattern. Neaten the ends of the strips with scissors. Take care that the strips are still securely in place.

⑤ Cut a piece of white card 13 x 12 cm (5 x 4¾ in). Use double-sided tape to attach over the back of the strip pattern.

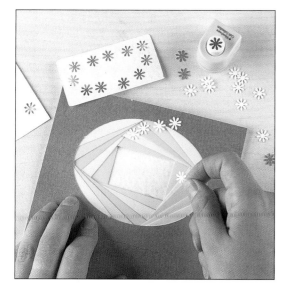

⑥ Turn the card over and you will see that the pattern is now complete. Punch out 12 white daisies and 3 blue daisies using the remaining pieces of card. Use PVA glue to attach the daisies. You can make up your own design or follow the layout in the photo opposite.

⑦ Use yellow 3D paint to embellish the daisies.

Party invitations

A colourful, fun sheet of gift-wrap was my inspiration for this project. Creating borders from gift-wrap is an effective way to decorate paper or a card. The pattern on the gift-wrap is quite similar to the balloon shapes and it co-ordinates well. Decorating envelopes takes a little time but gives the project a professional finish.

YOU WILL NEED

Pencil
Ruler
4 A4 (210 x 297 mm/
    8¼ x 11¾ in) sheets
    white paper
Paper trimmer
Small oval cutter (the
    oval should be 3 cm/
    1¼ in wide and 4 cm/
    1½ in high)
A5 (148 x 210 mm/
    5¾ x 8¼ in) sheets of
    green, red, blue paper
Sheet suitable gift-wrap
Glue stick
Black and coloured felt-
    tip pens
Scissors
6 C6 (114 x 162 mm/
    4½ x 6⅜ in) envelopes

1 Mark up and cut three of the A4 sheets of white paper to make six sheets of paper 13 x 19 cm (5 x 7½ in). Use the oval cutter to cut oval shapes for the balloons from the green, red and blue paper, six of each colour. Prepare the borders using the gift-wrap. Cut 12 strips 0.7 x 12.5 cm (⅜ x 5 in) long and 12 strips 0.7 x 16.5 cm (⅜ x 6½ in) long. The easiest way to do this is using a paper trimmer, but use a metal ruler, craft knife and cutting mat if you don't have one.

2 Take one of the sheets of white paper. Mark up the centre of the width of the sheet, 3 cm (1¼ in) from the top. Using the glue stick, attach a blue and a green balloon on either side of the pencil point, placing them at a slight angle. Glue a red balloon in a central position slightly higher than the other balloons. Using a black felt-tip pen, draw a wiggly line down from each balloon to create the effect of a string.

3 Take the gift-wrap strips and attach them with the glue stick just in from the edge of the sheet. Cut the strip to go at the top of the page to allow for the balloons, ensure that the ends are tucked in under the balloons. This strip should be positioned so that it sits centrally either side of the balloons.

④ Cut away the paper around the balloons, leaving a narrow border. Repeat steps 2–4 for the rest of the sheets.

⑤ Using a coloured felt-tip pen, rule lines on the sheets, approximately 1 cm (½ in) apart.

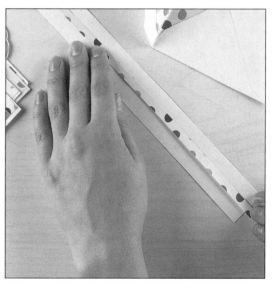

⑥ To decorate the envelopes, cut a piece of gift-wrap that will fit inside the envelope, within the sticky edge of the flap. Tuck it inside the envelope. (You will only need enough gift-wrap to show within the visible area of the open envelope it does not need to go down all the way to the bottom.) Use a glue stick to hold the gift-wrap in place.

⑦ Make a holder for your party invitations from a 3 cm (1¼ in) wide strip of A4 white paper. Embellish with a strip of gift-wrap glued centrally along the strip of white paper. Pile the writing paper and envelopes together, then wrap the strip around the stationery and glue the strip together at the back. Punch out three more balloon shapes and stick them across the join.

Easter eggs in a woven basket

Paper weaving is a very simple but extremely effective technique and an obvious method to use for creating a basket. I love making Easter cards, as you can use all of the fresh, bright colours of spring. Have fun decorating your Easter eggs!

YOU WILL NEED

A5 (148 x 210 mm/
  5¾ x 8¼ in) sheet
  spring green card
Scrap paper
Pencil
Low-tack adhesive tape
A5 (148 x 210 mm/
  5¾ x 8¼ in) sheet
  brown paper
Scissors
Craft knife/cutting mat
PVA (craft) glue
Glue stick
3D sticky foam pads
Oval cutter 2 x 3 cm
  (¾ x 1¼ in) (or use
  template on page 153)
A5 (148 x 210 mm/
  5¾ x 8¼ in) sheets of
  green, yellow, pink,
  pale blue, brown,
  shimmer blue paper
Selection of suitable
  printed papers
Small flower cutter
Deckle-edged scissors
3D paint in yellow,
  pink, blue
Green gel pen
Daffodil punch
Butterfly punch

1   Fold the green card in half to form the card blank. Trace the basket template on page 153 on to scrap paper. Tape the template on to the brown paper. Use scissors to cut along the marked lines – you will be weaving through these cut strips. Cut four ribbon strips of brown paper 15 x 0.5 cm (6 x ⅕ in).

2   Weave the ribbon strips between the cut strips. Thread the first ribbon strip over the cut strips, the second under the cut strips; the third strip over and the fourth strip under (see page 23). Use a dot of PVA glue to hold the ends of the ribbon strips in place.

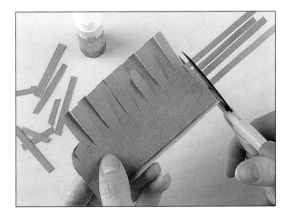

3   Use the basket template again, this time you just need the outline basket shape. Cut this shape out of brown paper. Use a glue stick to attach the piece of weaving to the basket shape, aligning the two top straight edges. Be sure to put plenty of glue on the strips. Trim off the excess strips and shape the weaving, using the base basket shape as a guide. Fold the top of the basket over and hold in place with 3D sticky foam pads.

④ Using 3D sticky foam pads, stick the basket in place on the card blank – it should be central, towards the bottom (note that the card is landscape). To make the handle, cut a strip of brown paper 13 x 1 cm (5 x ½ in). Fold in half. Tuck the ends of the handle under the basket and use PVA glue to hold in place. Glue the top of the handle in place also.

⑤ Now make the Easter eggs. You will need six ovals 2 x 3 cm (¾ x 1¼ in) cut out of the different coloured papers. Basically you can decorate the eggs however you like, here are some ideas and look at the image on page 57 for more: tiny punched flowers, strips of paper to look like ribbon, layer a slightly smaller oval on top and cut the edge with decorative scissors to give the impression of icing. Use a glue stick to attach three of the eggs to the card, tucking them inside the basket. Use 3D sticky foam pads to attach the remaining three eggs.

▼ **An alternative design using many of the elements from the main project, but in a different way.**

⑥ Finally punch out four green daffodils and four bright yellow daffodils. Cut the flowerheads off the yellow daffodils and stick them over the green heads. Attach the daffodils to the front and sides of the basket– half with PVA glue and half with 3D sticky foam pads. Paint a dot of yellow 3D paint in the centre of each flowerhead. Finally punch out two butterflies – one from blue paper and the other from yellow paper. Stick one on top of the other and stick to the front of the basket.

Embossed flowers
with watercolours

This card has an old-fashioned charm to it. Embossing is a gentle art and creates quite lovely images. The embossing takes place on the reverse of the image, pushing the image to the fore. Here I have decorated the embossed flowers with watercolour paints but you may prefer to use felt-tip pens or pencil crayons. (The main project is on the left of the image on page 59.)

YOU WILL NEED

A5 (148 x 210 mm/
  5¾ x 8¼ in) sheet pale
  green card
Ruler
Pencil
Eraser
Heart and flowers
  embossing stencil
Lightbox (optional)
Embossing tool
Fine paintbrush
Watercolour paints
Scrap of white paper

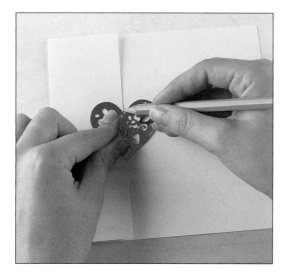

1 Place the sheet of green paper in front of you, longest side horizontal to you. Measure, along the top edge, the width of the paper and mark the central point. Rule a very light vertical line from this point to the bottom edge. Fold first one vertical side of the card, and then the other to this central line. Open up the card and erase the pencil line. Find the centre point of the central panel of the card using the stencil.

2 Embossing is done on the reverse side, so turn the card over. If you have one, place the stencil on the lightbox and put the sheet of card on top in the correct place. Use the embossing tool to emboss the design, you need to press quite firmly. If you don't have a lightbox, emboss on an old book, magazine, mousemat – a surface with a bit of give in it. You'll have to intermittently hold the card up to the light to check the progress of the design.

③ Still working on the reverse of the card, emboss a random flower pattern along the edges of the card flaps using a section of the stencil pattern. Move the stencil as you go and create a pretty pattern.

④ When you are happy with your embossed design, turn the card over. Using a fine paintbrush and watercolour paints, paint the raised surfaces of the flowers and leaves.

⑤ Use the stencil as a template to cut a heart shape out of white paper. Cut out the centre of the heart to create a frame. Use PVA glue to position it around the flower design on the central panel to highlight it.

Daffodils

In this card flowers are cut out and shaped from thin card. Simple shapes are used to form little daffodils standing in the centre of the card. Choose your colours well to create a pretty springtime display.

YOU WILL NEED

A5 (148 x 210 mm/
5¾ x 8¼ in) sheet
white card

A5 (148 x 210 mm/
5¾ x 8¼ in) sheet blue
paper

Pencil

Ruler

Glue stick

Scissors

A6 (105 x 148 mm/
4 x 8¼ in) sheets of
card: 1 butter-yellow,
1 bright yellow,
1 orange, 1 green

PVA (craft) glue

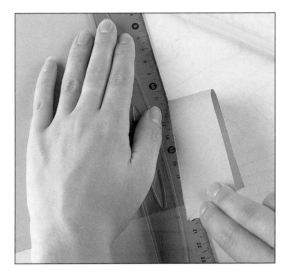

1 Fold the sheet of white card in half to form the card blank. Take the blue paper and measure a 4 cm (1½ in) wide strip down the longest side; use pencil dots to mark it. Line a ruler up with the pencil dots and tear off the strip. Open up the card blank, with the exterior towards you. Use a glue stick to attach the strip of blue paper across the whole card, front and back, in an upper central position approximately 5 cm (2 in) from the top.

▼ **This close-up shows the flowerhead of the daffodil in detail. The petals are shaped to give a three-dimensional effect.**

2 Using the templates on page 63, cut out one flower in butter-yellow card and two in bright yellow card. Cut three flower centres from orange card and follow the folding and cutting instructions on the template.

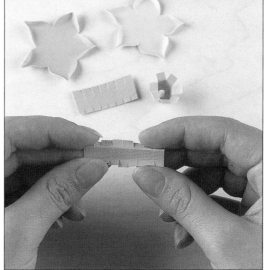

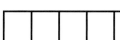

3 To shape the flowers you will need to hold each flower petal individually with your finger and thumb and use the fingers on your other hand to shape the petal up around the edges. Repeat with each petal.

4 Form each flower centre into a ring and glue the ends together using PVA glue. Fold the lower fringe inwards and the upper fringe outwards.

Flower centre

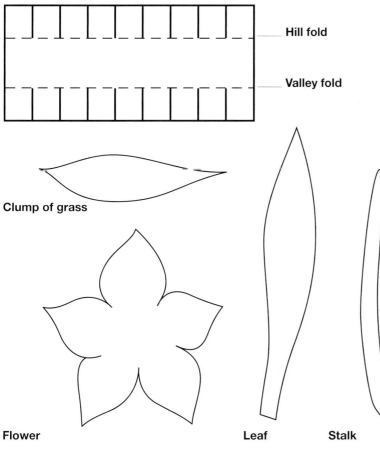

Hill fold

Valley fold

Clump of grass

Flower

Leaf

Stalk

5 Use the templates shown left to cut three leaves, three stalks and the clump of grass from green card. Attach them to the front of the card, using the image on page 62 as a guide. Attach the flowers and glue each centre in place. Stick on the clump of grass.

New baby pram

This card is so pretty and is irresistibly cute. Use floral or gingham paper to create the pram, perhaps depending on whether the baby is a boy or a girl. I cut the pram shape using an oval cutter. If you don't have one use the template below or design your own. I've used a daisy punch to great effect on this card, using it for the flowers and the wheel spokes.

YOU WILL NEED

A5 (148 x 210 mm/
    5¾ x 8¼ in) sheet pale
    green card
Oval cutter, 5 x 4 cm
    (2 x 1½ in)
A5 (148 x 210 mm/
    5¾ x 8¼ in) sheet
    white card
A5 (148 x 210 mm/
    5¾ x 8¼ in) sheet floral
    paper
Scrap of silver card
Punches: circle – 1.5 cm
    (⅝ in) diameter, daisy
    and leaf
A5 (148 x 210 mm/
    5¾ x 8¼ in) sheet
    green paper
Metal ruler
Craft knife
Cutting mat
Glue stick
Scissors
Decorative scissors
Pink 3D paint
3D sticky foam pads

① Fold the pale green card to form the card blank. Cut the oval out of white card and floral paper. Punch two circles out of white card. Cut a 2-mm (¹⁄₁₆ in) wide strip of silver card 2 cm (¾ in) long. Punch out the following: two daisies from silver card, five daisies from floral paper, five leaf stalks from green paper.

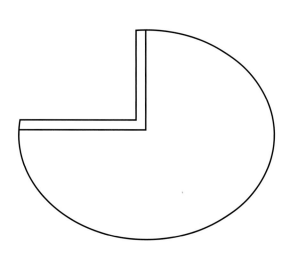

② Cut a narrow strip of green paper 10 cm (4 in) long. Glue it centrally on the card, about 2 cm (¾ in) up from the base. Stick one of the leaf stalks centrally along the green strip.

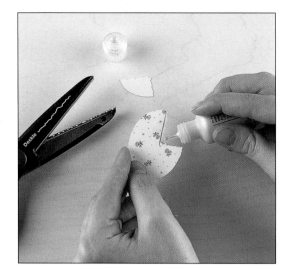

▼ **This close-up shows how simple shapes and patterns combine to make an effective card design.**

3 Prepare the pram body: cut out approximately a quarter of the floral paper oval. Glue this on to the white card oval. Now cut out a quarter of the white card oval with the decorative scissors – cut 2 mm (1/16 in) away from the floral oval so as to leave a white border. Paint a line of pink 3D paint along the decorative edge – this gives the impression of a frill. Leave to dry.

4 Use 3D sticky foam pads to attach the following: the pram should sit centrally, just on top of the leaf stalk; one wheel either side of the leafy stalk; the pram handle.

5 Stick the remaining stalks in place and four floral paper daisies using a glue stick. Attach the two silver daisies centrally on the wheels. Embellish all of the daisies with a spot of pink 3D paint.

Pop-up wedding cake

This is the simplest of pop-up cards. The pop-ups are created using simple rectangles of thin card. Accuracy in measuring and cutting out is essential. Once you have mastered the art you can create your own pop-up designs.

YOU WILL NEED

2 A5 (148 x 210 mm/
    5¾ x 8¼ in) sheets
    white card
Metal ruler
Embossing tool
Cutting mat
Craft knife
A4 (210 x 297 mm /
    8¼ x 11¾ in) sheet
    pale spangled blue
    gossamer paper or
    tissue paper
Scissors
Aerosol glue
Decorative scissors
A6 (105 x 148 mm/
    4 x 8¼ in) sheet silver
    card
Embossing pen
Silver embossing
    powder
Scrap paper
Precision heat tool
    (see page 13)
PVA (craft) glue
Embossing pad
Champagne glass
    rubber stamp
Yellow felt-tip pen
9 tiny diamond jewels

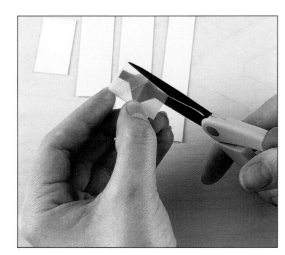

1 Score and fold one of the sheets of white card to form the card blank. Cut the sheet of spangled blue gossamer paper or tissue paper in half, to get an A5 sheet. Use aerosol glue to stick it to the inside of the card blank. Using the templates on page 154, cut out the elements for the cake pop-up out of white card.

2 Use an embossing tool to score all of the pop-up pieces as indicated. Use decorative scissors to cut along one edge of the longest piece. This piece represents the table on which the cake sits.

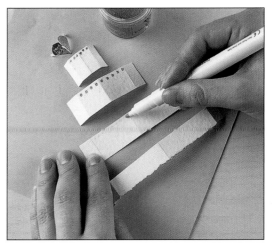

3 To embellish the pop-up pieces use an embossing pen and silver embossing powder. Work on a piece of scrap paper. Use the embossing pen to cover the heart, draw dots on the cake tiers and run it along the decorative edge of the 'table'. Sprinkle silver embossing powder over the pieces, then shake off any excess and return to the pot. Set the powder with the precision heat tool.

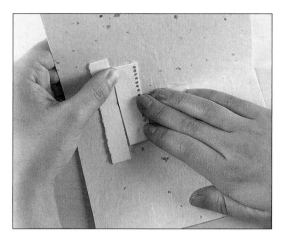

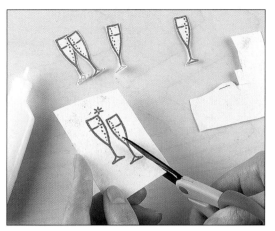

④ Open the card blank. Place a small amount of PVA glue on the tabs of the 'table' piece and stick it down on the card 2 cm (¾ in) up from the base of the card, ensuring that the centre fold is lined up with the centre fold of the card. Stick the rest of the pieces in place, leaving a small gap between them.

⑤ Using the embossing pad and champagne glass rubber stamp, make six impressions of the glass on white card. Working on scrap paper, sprinkle the stamped image with embossing powder, shake off the excess and seal with the precision heat tool. Cut out the glasses, and use PVA glue to attach two glasses on either side of the cake.

⑥ To decorate the front of the card cut a piece of white card 6 x 8 cm (2½ x 3¼ in) and a piece of spangled blue gossamer paper 6 x 8 cm (2½ x 3¼ in). Attach the gossamer paper to the white card. Use PVA glue to attach this to a piece of silver card 7 x 8 cm (2¾ x 3¼ in). Glue the layered card to the front of the card blank in an upper central position. Glue two champagne glasses to the front of the card. Embellish all of the champagne glasses by colouring in a little yellow to represent champagne. Place three diamond jewels above each set of glasses, both on the front and inside of the card to represent champagne bubbles.

TIPS

TO MAKE A GOOD POP-UP CARD YOU NEED TO MEASURE WITH PRECISION AND CREATE SHARP FOLDS. WHILE IT IS QUITE POSSIBLE TO USE DOUBLE-SIDED ADHESIVE TAPE TO FIX POP-UP ELEMENTS IN PLACE, I FIND THAT PVA GLUE IS BETTER AS IT CREATES A MORE PERMANENT FIXING.

IF YOU CAN'T FIND THE DIAMOND JEWELS, USE A GEL PEN TO DRAW ON THE BUBBLES.

TRY MAKING THIS CARD USING DIFFERENT COLOURS AND TEXTURES. I THINK IT WOULD LOOK LOVELY MADE UP IN A HANDMADE PAPER FOR EXAMPLE.

Table napkin daisies

Paper napkins and tissues can be used as a novel and fairly simple way of decorating paper and card. I chose this daisy napkin with a three-dimensional design in mind. The pattern makes a good background and when cut out the daisies work well together as a bunch.

YOU WILL NEED

A4 (210 x 297 mm/
  8¼ x 11¾ in) sheet
  white card
Metal ruler
Pencil
Craft knife
Cutting mat
Embossing tool
Suitable decorated
  table napkin or paper
  handkerchief
Aerosol glue
A4 (210 x 297 mm/
  8¼ x 11¾ in) sheet thin
  white card
Scissors
PVA (craft) glue
3D sticky foam pads
Piece green card 9.5 x
  6.5 cm (3¾ x 2¾ in)
Piece yellow card 10 x
  7 cm (4 x 2¾ in)

1 Cut the sheet of white card in half to create an A5 sheet. Set one piece aside. Score and fold the other piece in half to create the card blank. Separate out the individual napkin layers. Generally speaking, paper napkins are made up of three layers, and you will be using the decorative top layer only. Discard the other layers.

2 Cut a 13 x 14 cm (5 x 5½ in) piece out of the napkin. Spray the reverse of the napkin with aerosol glue and then place the napkin carefully over the front of the card blank, round to the back. Smooth the napkin as you go. There will be a little excess tissue paper to cut away. Stick the rest of the napkin layer onto the A4 sheet of thin white card using aerosol glue. This will be used for the central design on the front of the card.

▼ The daisies work
well in the three-
dimesional design
as they are a
simple, bold shape.
Try making the card
using a different
flower that is
similarly striking.

③ To make the design for the front of the card cut out a group of daisies. Glue this group to a piece of white card 9 x 6 cm (3½ x 2½ in) (using the card set aside in step 1). Using some of the green areas on the napkins cut out a small rectangle to use for the flower stems. Make cuts at the bottom of the rectangle. Glue this beneath the flowers.

④ Cut out about six or seven more daisies and layer them on the design using 3D sticky foam pads to form the posy of flowers.

⑤ Create a frame for the image, first layering it on to the green card and then the yellow. Attach the framed picture in a central position on the front of the card. You may want to glue a single daisy on the back of the card as a finishing touch.

Cupcakes

Cupcakes are great to eat and they're a fun motif for a card. Here I have designed a simple motif made up from different types of paper and card. The shapes are simple but it is the colours and variety of paper and card, as well as the embellishment, that create the interest.

YOU WILL NEED

A5 (148 x 210 mm/
   5¾ x 8¾ in) sheet violet
   card
Metal ruler
Pencil
Craft knife
Cutting mat
Embossing tool
A5 (148 x 210 mm/
   5¾ x 8¾ in) card
   sheets: 1 white,
   1 floral, 1 green,
   1 pink, 1 blue
Glue stick
Scissors
A5 (148 x 210 mm/
   5¾ x 8¾ in) sheet white
   corrugated card
Embossing pad
Scrap paper
White embossing
   powder
Precision heat tool
   (see page 13)
PVA (craft) glue
Flower punch
White 3D paint
C6 (114 x 162 mm/4½ x
   6⅜ in) violet envelope

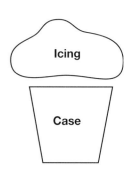

1 Cut a 14 x 15 cm (5½ x 6 in) piece of violet card. Score and fold it in half to form the card blank. Measure up and cut out three 3.5 cm (1½ in) squares from the floral card. Use a glue stick to attach the floral squares to the sheet of white card. Cut around the floral squares, leaving a narrow border (around 2 mm/¹⁄₁₆ in).

Icing

Case

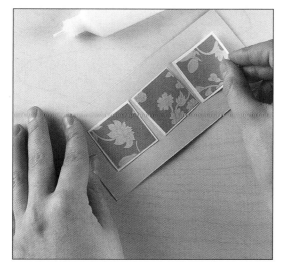

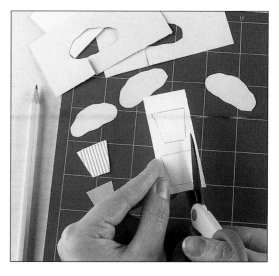

2 Stick the three bordered floral squares one above the other on the card. Place them at a slight angle, making sure that the middle square is centrally positioned on the card.

3 Now make the cupcakes. Using the template above, cut three cupcake cases from white corrugated card and three pieces of icing – one pink, one green and one blue.

4 Press one side of each piece of icing on to the embossing pad. Working on scrap paper, sprinkle each piece with white embossing powder and shake off the excess. Seal with the precision heat tool.

5 Use PVA glue to attach a cupcake case centrally on each floral square then place the piece of icing on top. Punch out three flowers and stick one on each cake. Embellish each flower with a single dot of 3D paint.

6 Decorate an envelope with punched-out flowers embellished with 3D paint.

▲ **The cupcake shape can be used in a number of different ways to create fun cards. Try enlarging the template. This card has a single cupcake topped with a birthday candle.**

Red roses

Making paper flowers may seem a fiddly occupation but the rewards make it well worthwhile.
An afternoon or evening spent creatively punching, folding and sticking can result in a selection
of flowers that will make great decorations for cards. These little roses look equally good made
in red or white, pink or orange. Choose whichever colour you prefer. Use the roses to embellish
cards, gift tags or even a gift box.

YOU WILL NEED

Pencil
Metal ruler
A5 (148 x 210 mm/
    5¾ x 8¼ in) sheet red
    card
Craft knife
Cutting mat
Embossing tool
A6 (105 x 148 mm/
    4 x 8¼ in) sheet
    parchment
Double-sided adhesive
    tape
A6 (105 x 148 mm/
    4 x 8¼ in) sheet green
    card
Embossing pad
White embossing
    powder
Precision heat tool
    (see page 13)
Medium flower punch
Scissors
PVA (craft) glue
Leaf punch
Scissors
Quilling tool
3D paint in green and
    white

1 Cut a 10.5 x 21 cm (4¼ x 8½ in) rectangle out of the red card. Score and fold in half to form the card blank (reserve the rest of the card for use in step 2). Cut out a 7 cm (2¾ in) square of parchment. Place a small piece of double-sided tape centrally on the parchment square and stick the square on to the centre of the card blank. Cut out a 3 cm (1¼ in) square of green card. Press the edges of the square on to the embossing pad. Then dip each edge into white embossing powder. Seal the powder with the precision heat tool.

2 Use double-sided tape to attach the square diagonally on the parchment so it forms a diamond shape. To make the paper roses, punch nine medium flower shapes out of red card. Place them in piles of three. Take a sharp pair of scissors and cut in a little (approx. 2 mm/¹⁄₁₆ in) at the indentation between each petal.

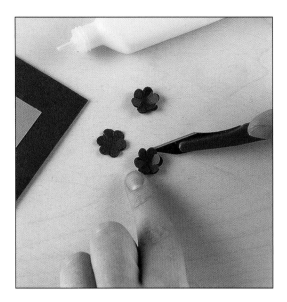

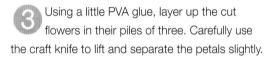

3 Using a little PVA glue, layer up the cut flowers in their piles of three. Carefully use the craft knife to lift and separate the petals slightly.

4 Cut three strips of red card 3 cm (1¼ in) long and 2 mm (⅟₁₆ in) wide. Using the quilling tool, roll them up into tightly quilled rolls. Use a dot of PVA glue to hold in place and glue one in the centre of each flower. Cut the stem piece 4 mm (⅛ in) wide and 2.5 cm (1 in) long from green card. Snip carefully to divide the piece of card into three stems, do not cut to the top.

5 First stick the stem piece on to the green square, then glue the three flowers in place. Now cut three simple leaves from green card and glue between the flowers.

6 Decorate the corners with 3D paint – a dot of green in each corner with three white dots either side.

Christmas tree

This stylishly shaped card is relatively quick and easy to make. The embossed green edging reminds us that Christmas trees are usually green and the randomly placed star cut-outs are like twinkling lights. The stickers are a little different and add Christmas magic to a card that would certainly stand out in any display.

YOU WILL NEED

A5 (148 x 210 mm/
 5¾ x 8¼ in) sheet white
 card
Pencil
Embossing tool
Scissors
Scallop-edging scissors
Embossing pen
Green embossing
 powder
Precision heat tool
 (see page 13)
Star hand punch
Christmas decoration
 and star stickers
White circular sticky
 label (see tip on
 page 80)

1 Trace and cut out the tree template on page 154. Place the template on to the sheet of white card and draw around it lightly. Cut out and use the embossing tool to score along the fold lines.

2 Take the scallop-edging scissors and cut along the bottom edge of the card. (Practise on some scrap paper first to ensure you have the scissors the right way up.)

3 Carefully run the embossing pen along the scalloped edge. Working on scrap paper, sprinkle the edge with green embossing powder, shake off the excess and seal with the precision heat tool.

4 Fold one flap over along the fold lines and use the star hand punch to cut out stars randomly. Fold in the flap from the other side and do the same, checking on the centre panel that you're spacing the stars satisfactorily.

5 Decorate the tree with Christmas decoration stickers and a star at the top.

Lucky black cats

I have two lovely black cats so when I found these peel-offs I was inspired, as you can see! Peel-offs and punches give this pop-up card a very professional finish. I used coloured cards with various textures to create the different elements. Make a selection of pots decorated with different flowers and save some for another time – it is a lovely and useful motif. You might want to have a practice run with plain white card to see how the pop-up works before you work on the actual card.

YOU WILL NEED

A5 (148 x 210 mm/
   5¾ x 8¼ in) sheet white
   card
Pencil
Metal ruler
Embossing tool
Tracing paper
Eraser
Sheets of different
   textured card in green,
   blue, brick-brown,
   terracotta-brown,
   black
PVA (craft) glue
Flowerpot and leaf
   punches
Adhesive tape
Sheet flower stickers
3D sticky foam pads
Double-sided tape
Black cat peel-offs

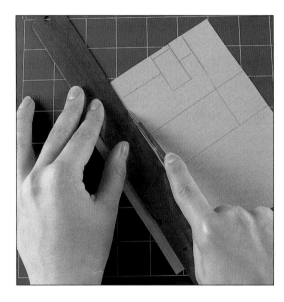

TIP

REFER TO THE IMAGE ON PAGE 83. THE TWO CARDS IN THE BACKGROUND SHOW HOW THE ELEMENTS USED IN THE MAIN PROJECT CAN BE APPLIED TO A VERY SIMPLE DECORATIVE DESIGN. OBVIOUSLY THESE CARDS WOULD BE QUICKER TO MAKE THAN THE POP-UP DESIGN.

---

1 Score and fold the sheet of white card to make the card blank. Trace the template on page 155 onto the sheet of green card. Cut out, score and fold. Erase any pencil marks.

2 Open up the card blank (remember that this card is landscape). The template on page 155 shows the areas of the pop-up that are glued to the card blank. Apply PVA glue to these areas, but on the reverse of the pop-up. Glue the pop-up in place, ensuring that the two valley folds on line A, sit in the central fold of the card blank.

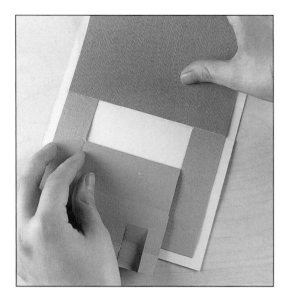

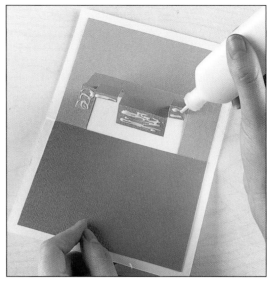

3 Measure and cut out a piece of blue card 13.5 x 9.5 cm (5¼ x 3¾ in). Use PVA glue to stick the blue card in place, lining it up with the edges of the pop-up.

4 Place PVA glue on all the areas of the pop-up that are to be stuck to the blue card. This time the glue is placed on the right side of the pop-up, as these flaps are then folded downwards. Stick to the blue card.

5 For the brick wall cut strips of brick-brown coloured card 9 mm (½ in) wide. Trim into 1.5 cm (⅝ in) long pieces and use PVA glue to attach them. Bear in mind that you should leave a small space above and below the folds to enable them to operate.

6 To make the pots of flowers punch out nine flowerpots from terracotta-brown card and plenty of single leaves from green card. Cut a 2 cm (¾ in) length of adhesive tape and attach it 1 cm (½ in) down the back of the pot, with the other centimetre sticking up. Attach four leaves on to the adhesive tape. Stick a group of flowers on top of the leaves. Make up all of the flowerpots in this way.

◀ **This photo shows the front of the pop-up card.**

7. Stick eight of the pots in place – some with 3D sticky foam pads and some with double-sided adhesive tape – arrange them carefully as you would pots of flowers in your own garden.

8. Make three other groupings of flowers and leaves. Stick them all in place with double-sided adhesive tape – one to the wall and the other two on the green card. Stick two of the same design black cat peel-offs together. Use 3D sticky foam pads to stick the black cat in place. To complete the card, attach the remaining flowerpot centrally to a piece of blue card 10.5 x 5 cm (4¼ x 2 in). Layer this on to a black sheet of card. Use a craft knife to cut away the excess black card leaving a narrow border. Attach the framed picture to a 13 x 8 cm (5 x 3¼ in) piece of green card and attach the picture centrally on the front of the card.

Three apple trees

This simple design looks sophisticated and stylish. Large, loosely quilled coils make up the trees' foliage, tight coils represent the apples and the trunk is a tightly rolled square of brown paper.

1 Cut a rectangle of blue card 17.5 x 15 cm (6¾ x 6 in). Using the template on page 156, score, fold and cut the centre as indicated. Set aside. If you don't have quillling paper, cut 2 cm (¾ in) wide strips, the length of the A4 sheet: 12 of green paper and 30 of pink. Cut three 4 x 6 cm (1½ x 2½ in) rectangles of brown paper.

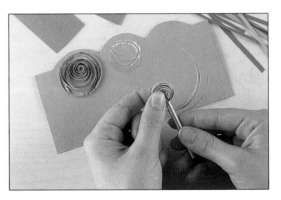

2 Load the quilling tool with four strips of green paper and coil. Release the coil into a more open spiral to make the tree foliage. Use dots of PVA glue to hold the ends in place. Put some PVA glue onto the blue card where the tree foliage sits and stick the coil in place. Make two more like this and stick in place.

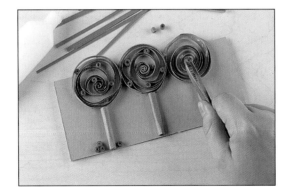

3 Trim the strips of pink paper to 18 cm (7 in) in length. Coil each strip into a tight spiral and glue the ends. Stick six pink coils in each tree. From the short side, roll each rectangle of brown paper into a tube. Glue in place. Stick four pink coils around the base of each tree.

4 Glue the decorated blue card on to a sheet of green card. Use a craft knife and ruler to cut away all but a 1 mm (¹⁄₃₂ in) green border. Layer this on to pink card. Repeat as above but this time leave a 2 mm (¹⁄₁₆ in) wide border.

Flower collage

The stamp I used for this project has eight different motifs each contained within a decorative square. You could use the stamped image as a whole, but I decided to use each of the motifs individually to make this card. You may want to have a few practice runs with the stamp on some rough paper before beginning work on the card proper.

YOU WILL NEED

A4 (210 x 297 mm/
  8¼ x 11¾ in) sheet
  dark blue card
Metal ruler
Craft knife
Cutting mat
Embossing tool
Suitable rubber stamp/s
A5 (148 x 210 mm/
  5¾ x 8¼ in) sheet white
  card
Embossing pad
Scrap paper
Gold embossing
  powder
Precision heat tool
  (see page 13)
Felt-tip pens in gold,
  fuchsia, dark blue,
  green
PVA (craft) glue
Scissors
A5 (148 x 210 mm/
  5¾ x 8¼ in) sheet violet
  card
3D sticky foam pads
Scrap of green card
Punches: medium and
  small flower, leafy stalk
Pink 3D paint

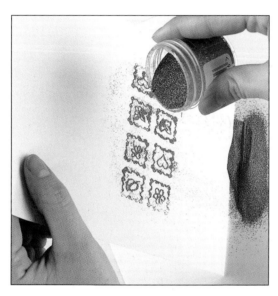

---

1 Cut a 22 x 10.5 cm (8½ x 4¼ in) rectangle out of the dark blue card (keep the offcuts for use later). Fold in half to make the card blank. Stamp the image on to the white card using the embossing pad. Working on scrap paper, sprinkle the stamped image with gold embossing powder and seal with the precision heat tool.

2 Use a gold felt-tip pen to colour outside and in between the images, and to trace round the outline of the images. Use different coloured felt-tip pens to embellish the flowers, leaves and hearts. Use a craft knife and ruler to cut the stamped design into eight individual motifs.

TIPS

IF YOU CANNOT FIND A RUBBER STAMP LIKE THE ONE THAT I HAVE USED, SIMPLY USE INDIVIDUAL STAMPS TO CREATE THE MOTIFS.

INSTEAD OF USING STAMPED IMAGES YOU COULD USE STICKERS OR CUT OUT MOTIFS FROM GIFT-WRAP.

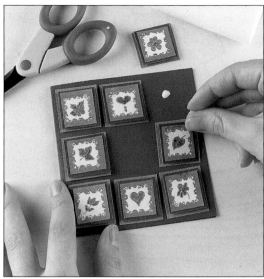

▼ **Viewed close-up you will see the embossed gold edging created by the stamp is most effective.**

3 Glue the motifs on to dark blue card, leaving a bit of space between each one. Use scissors to cut around the motifs, leaving a narrow blue border. Don't worry about the border being even, the card is supposed to have a handmade look. Attach the framed motifs to the sheet of violet card using 3D sticky foam pads. Leave space between each one, and cut out leaving a narrow border.

4 Now you are ready to assemble your card. Using glue, stick the framed motifs on to the card as shown. Punch out two large violet flowers, two small blue flowers and three green leafy stalks.

5 Use glue to stick one leafy stalk, violet and blue flower centrally on the back of the card. Do the same in the centre of the front of the card. Put another layer of these shapes on top, but with a 3D sticky foam pad in between. Embellish the dark blue flowers with a spot of pink 3D paint.

Retro flowers

This is one of my favourite designs. The card can be made in different colourways. If you do not have a retro print paper to hand use any floral paper gift-wrap or plain paper decorated with stamped images. Let your creativity run away with you!

YOU WILL NEED

Piece white card
  10 x 20 cm (4 x 8 in)
Metal ruler
Pencil
Embossing tool
Cutting mat
Craft knife
Floral retro print paper
Glue stick
A6 (105 x 148 mm/
  4 x 8¼ in) sheets card
  in green, white and
  turquoise
3D sticky foam pads
Punches: large flower,
  medium flower, small
  flower, small disc
  shape
Matte textured papers
  in blue, green
  and brown
PVA (craft) glue
3D paint in pale blue,
  green and yellow

1. Score and fold the white card to create the card blank. Cut a 10 x 11.5 cm (4 x 4½ in) piece of the floral paper to cover the front of the card. Apply glue to the reverse side of the floral paper and cover the front of the card, folding the excess around to the back of the card. Cut a 7.5 cm (3 in) square of green card. Glue it in a central position on the front of the card. Measure and cut out a 6 cm (2½ in) square of white card. Glue this square to the turquoise card. Use a craft knife to cut around the white card leaving a narrow frame of turquoise.

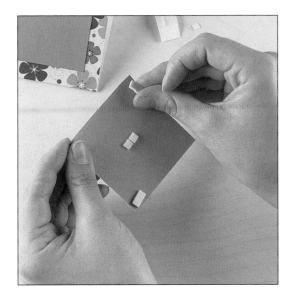

2. Attach the layered square centrally on the green card using 3D sticky foam pads.

3. Now you are ready to make the flowers. Referring to the photo on page 92, punch out a selection of flowers and discs in various sizes out of the textured papers.

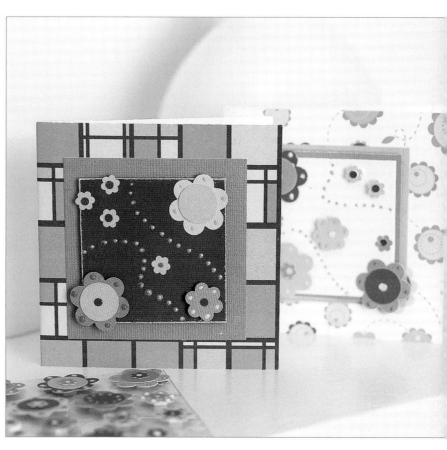

4 Use PVA glue to attach the various punched flowers and discs to one another.

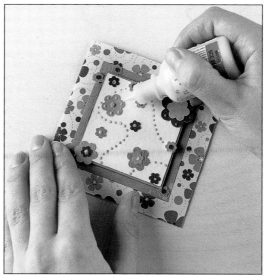

▲ **These cards have been constructed using the same technique, but different papers.**

5 Attach some of the flowers using glue and some with 3D sticky foam pads.

6 Embellish some of the flowers with dots of 3D paint and paint a trail of dots on the white card.

Wedding invitations and place settings

This simple elegant stamp has been used here to decorate invitations and place settings, but it could also be used on favour bags or boxes, order of ceremony sheets and thank-you notes for gifts. As it's important for wedding stationery to look perfect, practise first on some scrap paper. The instructions for the place settings are on page 96.

YOU WILL NEED

A4 (210 x 297 mm/
  8¼ x 11¾ in) sheet
  white, slightly textured
  card
Metal ruler
Pencil
Cutting mat
Craft knife
Low-tack adhesive tape
Eraser
Suitable rubber stamp
Embossing pad
Scrap paper
Silver embossing
  powder
Precision heat tool
  (see page 13)
Decorative scissors

1 Cut a rectangle of white card 10 x 20 cm (4 x 8 in). Lay the card on your work surface, long edge towards you. Measure the width of the card and find the centre. Mark this point at the top and bottom edge. Rule a light pencil line between the points. Fold one side of the card in to the centre line and then the other. Make sure the folds are sharp. Erase the pencil line. Close the folds over the centre and use a couple of pieces of low-tack tape at either edge to hold them closed.

2 Use low-tack tape to stick the card to a mat. Press the stamp onto the embossing pad, then press the stamp onto the card – positioning it centrally over the closed flaps. Remove all the tape. Holding the card over scrap paper, sprinkle with silver embossing powder. Shake off the excess. Seal the powder with the precision heat tool.

3 Hold the invitation closed. Cut along the top and bottom edges with the decorative scissors. Press the edges on to the embossing pad, then into embossing powder. Shake off the excess and seal with the precision heat tool. If you want to, rule some lines on the central panel of the card on which you can write your invite.

Wedding place settings

YOU WILL NEED

Cutting mat

Metal ruler

Pencil

Craft knife

Piece white card
  10 x 11 cm (4 x 4¼ in)

Embossing tool

Silver pen

Suitable rubber stamp

Silver embossing
  powder

Embossing pad

Precision heat tool (see
  page 13)

Scrap paper

Deckle-edged scissors

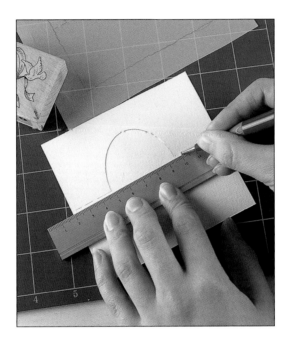

1 Follow the template guide on page 157 to mark up, score, fold and cut the piece of white card.

2 Open the piece of card out flat. Outline the edge of the oval with a silver pen. Stamp the design within the oval shape using the embossing pad. Working on scrap paper, sprinkle over the embossing powder, shake off the excess and seal with the precision heat tool. Fold the place setting. Cut around the edges with decorative scissors. Press the edges on to the embossing pad. Again, working on scrap paper, sprinkle over the embossing powder and shake off the excess. Seal with the precision heat tool.

New baby announcement card

I love this card. It is simple enough to make and very effective. The vellum I used is available in pink and blue, but you may want to choose a paper or an alternative decorated vellum.

YOU WILL NEED

A4 (210 x 297 mm/
 8¼ x 11¾ in) sheet
 white card

Suitable decorative
 vellum

Metal ruler

Pencil

Craft knife

Cutting mat

Embossing tool

Glue stick

Oval cutter

A4 (210 x 297 mm/
 8¼ x 11¾ in) sheet
 acetate

Rub-off transfers of
 baby hands and feet
 in silver

Adhesive tape

Deckle-edged scissors

▶ **The window effect is simple to make and highlighted with a deckle edge frame.**

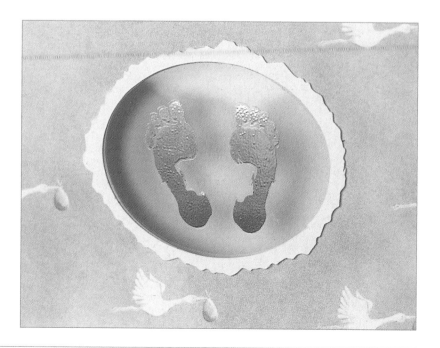

1 Begin by preparing the card blank. Take the white card and the decorative vellum. Measure up both and cut out sheets measuring 10 x 21 cm (4 x 8½ in). Score and fold the card in half. Use a glue stick to attach the decorative vellum to the white card blank.

2 Use a pencil and ruler to measure and mark up the centre point of the front of the card. To do this, place a ruler diagonally across the front of the card, corner to corner. Draw lines a couple of centimetres long with a pencil in either direction across the centre area. You will find that the cross formed will mark the centre. Use the oval cutter to cut out a 3 x 4-cm (1½ x 1½-in) oval window in the centre of the front of the card.

3 Measure and cut out a piece of acetate 4 x 6 cm (1½ x 2½ in). Transfer a pair of silver feet on to the acetate. To do this, you will need your embossing tool. Place the transfer on top of the acetate and, with the little feet in the centre of the acetate, rub away with your embossing tool until the transfer has attached itself firmly to the acetate. Use adhesive tape to attach the decorated acetate inside the window.

4 Next, you will need to make a frame for the little silver feet. Cut out an oval 4 x 6 cm (1½ x 2½ in) from white card. Use deckle-edged scissors to cut a decorative edge around the oval, 4 mm (¼ in) from the inner edge. Use a glue stick to attach the frame around the window. Write the baby's birth details on a slip of paper and tape into place. You might want to embellish an envelope with a little transfer of a pair of silver hands from the same transfer sheet.

Halloween

Peel-offs are a quick and easy way to create wonderfully professional-looking motifs. The seasonal images I have chosen are readily available but if you have difficulty in locating them use the templates on page 155 to cut out homemade pumpkins. The decoration would look equally good on Halloween party bags or invitations.

YOU WILL NEED

A4 (210 x 297 mm/
    8¼ x 11¾ in) sheet
    night-time blue sugar
    paper
Halloween pumpkin
    peel-offs, one with
    face markings
A5 (148 x 210 mm/
    5¾ x 8¼ in) sheets of
    yellow and orange
    card
Scissors
Craft knife
Cutting mat
PVA (craft) glue
Small piece black card
Double-sided tape
3D sticky foam pads
Small pieces of paper in
    shades of green,
    brown and orange
    (autumn colours)
Leaf punch

1 Fold the sheet of blue sugar paper into four to form the card blank. Stick two pumpkin peel-offs on to yellow card and one feature pumpkin on to orange card. Cut out the pumpkins, cutting out the face markings of the feature pumpkin.

2 Use PVA glue to attach a piece of black card behind the cut-out features of the feature pumpkin, to create an impression of hollowness.

3 Use double-sided tape to attach a large pumpkin off-centre on the front of the card and 3D sticky foam pads to attach the remaining pumpkins. Punch out a selection of autumn leaves from the green, brown and orange paper and use PVA glue to attach them in a random manner around the base of the pumpkins. Cut out two bats from black card using the template on page 155 and attach them above the pumpkins.

4/Gift Items

IT IS POSSIBLE TO MAKE LOVELY GIFTS FROM PAPER. IN THIS SECTION THERE ARE IDEAS AND INSTRUCTIONS FOR AN INTERESTING SELECTION OF ITEMS. SOME ARE QUICK AND EASY TO MAKE, LIKE THE FROG AND WATER LILIES BOOKMARK, OTHERS TAKE MORE TIME AND A LITTLE DEDICATION, LIKE THE CRANE MOBILE. THE MEMORY BOARD MAKES A PARTICULARLY LOVELY GIFT, IN THE EXAMPLE THE PHOTOGRAPH IS OF MY SISTER, GRANDMOTHER AND MYSELF, TAKEN IN 1958 BY ONE OF THOSE STREET PHOTOGRAPHERS THAT WERE ONCE SO POPULAR. IT WOULD BE GOOD TO MAKE IT WITH RECENT PHOTOGRAPHS OF CRAFTING FRIENDS USING EITHER VINTAGE OR MODERN MEMORABILIA. I HOPE YOU ARE INSPIRED TO MAKE THE PROJECTS AND LEARN A FEW NEW TECHNIQUES ALONG THE WAY!

Crane mobile

Origami is the traditional Japanese art of folding paper. Use origami paper, but practise with some scrap paper first.

YOU WILL NEED

Sixteen 15 cm (6 in) squares origami paper, for the cranes
Darning needle
Strong thread
Piece card 3 x 90 cm (1¼ x 36 in)
PVA (craft) glue
Paperclip or bulldog clip

① Make the cranes first following the diagrams and instructions below:

A Using one of the squares of origami paper, fold it in half top to bottom and diagonally.

B Fold along all four creases at the same time.

C Fold two edges in, to form a kite-shape on top.

D Do the same on the other side.

E Undo the folds you made in steps c and d.

F Pull the bottom corner (the top layer only) up above the top corner. Fold along the creases you made in steps c and d.

G Do the same thing on the other side. The top flaps are the wings and the bottom flaps are the neck and tail.

H Fold two edges in, as in step e.

I Do the same thing on the other side.

J Fold the top left flap to meet the top right flap. Fold the bottom right flap to meet the bottom left flap.

K Fold up the neck and the tail as far as you can.

L Fold the head down.

M Repeat step j.

N Pull the neck and tail out and down so they are not vertical.

O Pull the head out and up so it's not parallel to the neck.

P Pull the wings straight out from the body and blow through the hole in the underside so that the body inflates.

Make the other nine cranes in the same way.

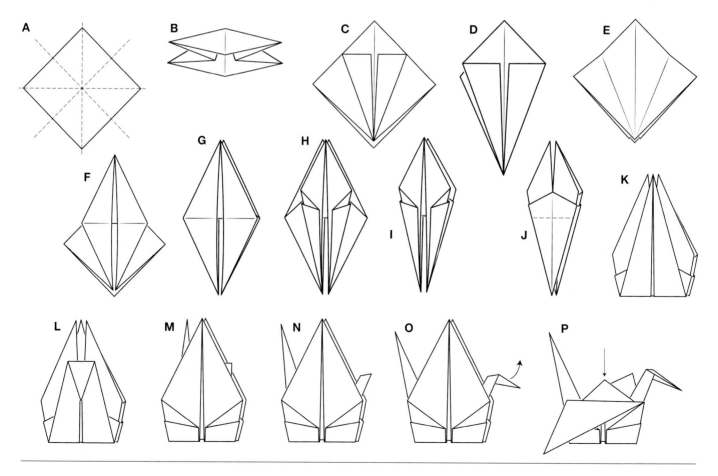

2 Once all the cranes are made you need to attach a length of thread to each one. Cut ten 50 cm (20 in) lengths of thread. Thread the darning needle with a length of thread. Make a large knot at one end. Thread the darning needle through the same hole you used to puff air into the crane's body. Push the needle through the centre of the crane's back. The knot should hold the thread in place. Attach a length of thread to each crane.

3 Next, make the mobile hanger. Take the piece of card and use PVA glue to stick the ends together to form a hoop, overlapping the card by 3 cm (1¼ in). Use a paperclip or bulldog clip to hold the hoop in place until the glue sets.

4 Cover the hoop with the remaining squares of origami paper, using PVA glue.

5 Rethread the darning needle with a length of thread with the crane attached. Push the needle through the hoop, pulling the thread through. Unthread the needle, and knot the end of the thread. Attach all of the cranes in this way, adjusting the lengths of the threads to create a mobile that hangs evenly.

Daisy bookmark

This bookmark is decorated with the simplest of geometric patterns. Simple triangle shapes are cut through the paper and decorated with daisies.

YOU WILL NEED

Pencil

Tracing paper

A5 (148 x 219 mm/
  5¾ x 8¼ in) sheet blue
  card

A5 (148 x 219 mm/
  5¾ x 8¼ in) sheet
  white paper

Cutting mat

Low-tack adhesive tape

Craft knife

Metal ruler

Scissors

Embossing tool

PVA (craft) glue

A5 (148 x 219 mm/
  5¾ x 8¼ in) sheet
  white card

Daisy punch

Yellow 3D paint

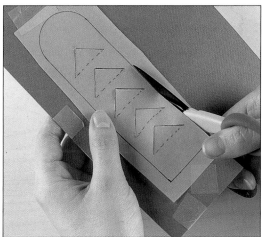

1 Trace the template of the front of the bookmark on page 157. Place the blue card exactly on top of the white paper and tape (at the corners) to a cutting mat. Place the template for the front of the bookmark on top of the card and tape to secure. Use a craft knife to cut two sides of each triangle, cutting through both the blue card and the white paper.

2 Once you have made all of the cuts on the triangles, cut out the outline of the bookmark. Keep the offcuts of blue card for use later. Remove the template.

3 Use a small amount of PVA glue in the corners to hold the blue and white bookmark layers in place. Score across the top of each triangle. Fold back each triangle. Put a dot of glue at the tip of each triangle (on the blue card side) and stick down.

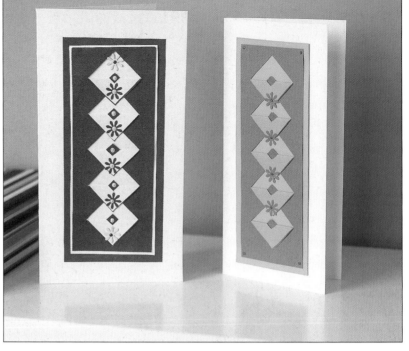

④ Glue the front of the bookmark on to the sheet of white card. Trim around the blue card, leaving a thin border. Alternatively, trace the template for the bookmark backing on page 157 and cut out of the white card. Glue the two layers together. Keep the offcuts of white card for use in step 5.

⑤ Punch out five blue daisies and five white daisies out of the offcuts of card.

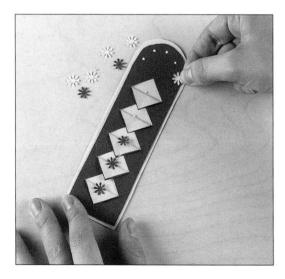

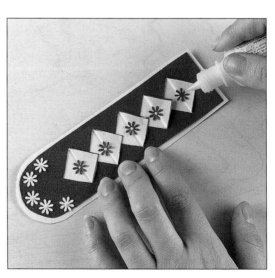

⑦ Embellish the flowers with yellow 3D paint.

⑥ Glue the daisies in place, one blue flower on each white fold and five white daisies around the top of the bookmark.

Kimono doll mobile

A friend brought me a sheaf of beautiful washi paper back from Japan. This paper is richly decorated in colours reminiscent of the silk fabrics from which kimonos are made. I thought it should be used in a project of a lasting nature, and this pretty mobile of little kimono dolls fits the bill perfectly. The lovely little kimono doll would look equally attractive decorating a birthday card or gift-box.

YOU WILL NEED

Pencil

Scissors

Ruler

9 A5 (148 x 219 mm/ 5¾ x 8¼ in) sheets washi paper

A5 (148 x 219 mm/ 5¾ x 8¼ in) white card

A5 (148 x 219 mm/ 5¾ x 8¼ in) black card

A5 (148 x 219 mm/ 5¾ x 8¼ in) sheets plain coloured paper

Embossing tool

Glue stick

PVA (craft) glue

Nine 30 cm (12 in) lengths blue thread

Nine 20 cm (8 in) lengths 8 mm (¼ in) wire

1 Cut out the pieces for the doll using the templates on page 158. To make each paper doll (there are 10 in total) you will need: one dress and two sleeves cut from washi paper, one face cut from white card and front and back hair cut from black card.

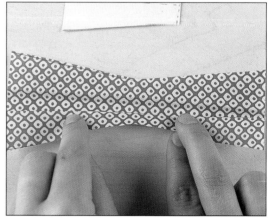

2 From plain coloured paper cut two rectangles 6.7 x 1.5 cm (2¾ x ½ in) for the sleeve trims and one 3.5 x 1.5 cm (1½ x ½ in) for the waistband. Use an embossing tool to score along the fold lines on the dress. Fold to create pleats. Fold in half to make the front and back of the dress.

3 Next, make the sleeves. Use a glue stick to attach the sleeve trim to the sleeve so that it protrudes slightly. Mark the folds as indicated and then fold into shape.

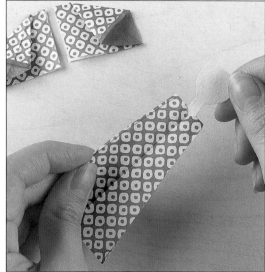

④ Continue folding until the sleeve is complete. Make sure the folds are sharp.

⑤ Cut a small central v-shape from the folded neck area of the dress. Slip the stem of the face piece into the hole. Place glue at the top of each sleeve and stick on either side of the body.

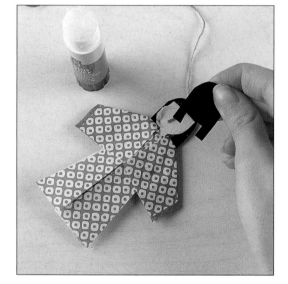

⑥ Glue the end of one length of blue thread running up from the back of the face and on top of that glue the hair front and back in place. Stick on the waistband. Make up the remaining eight paper dolls in the same way.

⑦ Bend each length of wire in half. Pinch a loop in the middle of the wire and open out. Bend up 0.5 cm (¼ in) at each end to create hooks. The dolls are hung from these hooks. To construct the mobile refer to the diagram on page 158.

Frogs and water lilies bookmark

Punched images are the feature on this little bookmark, which would make a good gift for a child. My colour choice is inspired by the Monet water lily paintings. Think about other paintings with vibrant colours and images that might inspire ideas. There is such a huge variety of punches available there's virtually no shape that you won't be able to find.

YOU WILL NEED

A5 (148 x 219 mm/
  5¾ x 8¼ in) sheet lime
  green thin card
Pencil
Metal ruler
Craft knife
Cutting mat
Punches: round corner,
  frog, small flower,
  medium flower, tiny
  butterfly
A5 (148 x 219 mm/
  5¾ x 8¼ in) sheet blue
  opaque paper
Scrap thin green thin
  card
Scrap pale green
  opaque paper
Scrap thin pink card
Double-sided adhesive
  tape
PVA (craft) glue
Sparkly green 3D paint

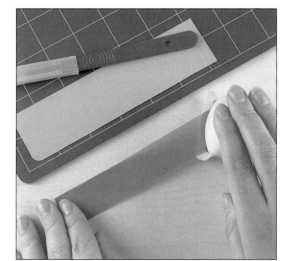

1 Prepare the bookmark base by measuring up and cutting out a rectangle of thin yellow card, 4 x 15.5 cm (1½ x 6¼ in). Use a corner punch to round the top corners of the bookmark. Set aside. Measure up and cut out a rectangle of blue opaque paper 2.5 x 14 cm (1 x 5½ in). Once again, use the corner punch to round the top corners.

2 Punch out five frogs from green card, five medium flowers from pale green opaque paper and five small flowers from pink card. Using double-sided tape, attach the strip of blue opaque paper centrally on the bookmark base. Use PVA glue to stick the frogs on to the bookmark in a staggered pattern.

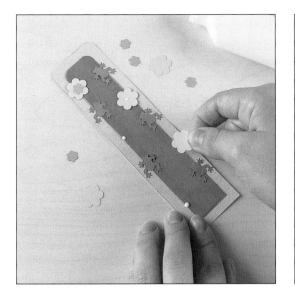

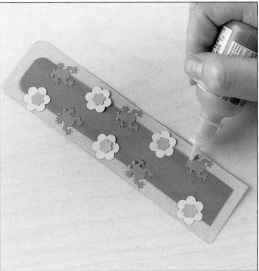

3 Stick the flowers, green first with a pink flower on top, in the spaces between the frogs.

4 Give the frogs eyes with spots of sparkly green 3D paint.

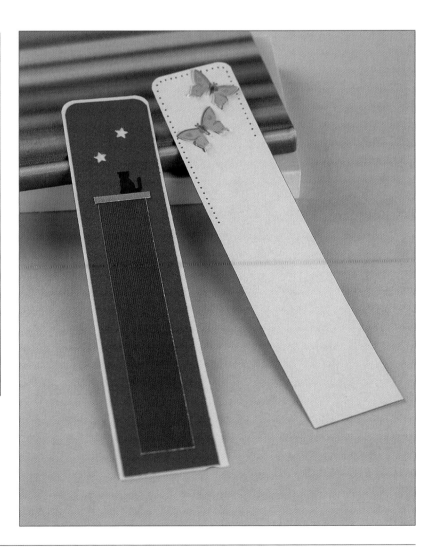

▶ **A couple of inspirational ideas for bookmarks constructed using punched-out shapes.**

Woven bookmark

I once sewed cushion covers decorated in a geometric tapestry pattern in these very colours. Purples, violets and greens go well together: lay the papers one beside the other to ensure that the shades work before you begin making your bookmark.

YOU WILL NEED

A4 (210 x 297 mm/
  8¼ x11¾ in) sheet thin
  purple card
Pencil
Metal ruler
Craft knife
Cutting mat
A4 (210 x 297 mm/
  8¼ x 11¾ in) sheets
  green and violet paper
PVA (craft) glue
Punches: round corner,
  daisy, butterfly
Scissors

1 Measure and cut out a rectangle of purple card 4 x 21 cm (1½ x 8½ in). Mark intervals of approximately 6 mm (¼ in) across the width of the bookmark at one end. Rule light pencil lines, 11.5 cm (4½ in) long, from these points. Cut these lines with a craft knife to create the fringe.

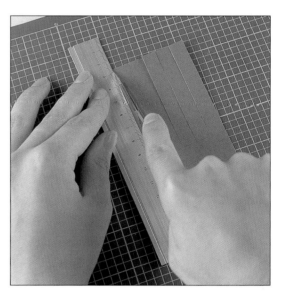

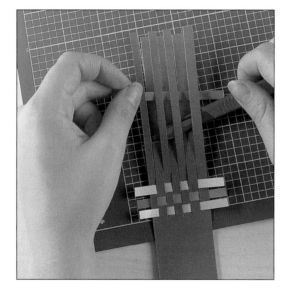

2 Cut five ribbons of green paper and four ribbons of violet paper measuring 5 x 0.5 cm (2 x ⅛ in). With the fringe end of the bookmark furthest away from you, begin to weave the paper ribbons through the cut strips. Start with green paper ribbon, weaving it under the fringe, then use a violet strip and weave it over the fringe. Continue like this until you have woven all of the ribbon strips in the fringe.

3 Fold the ribbon ends around to the back of the bookmark. Hold in place with glue.

4 Trim the corners with the corner punch. Using the daisy punch, cut out a single daisy at the top of the bookmark.

5 Use glue to attach the purple woven layer to a piece of green paper. Use a craft knife to cut around the bookmark, leaving a narrow frame of green paper. Use scissors to cut the green paper away beneath the fringed part of the bookmark.

6 Round the corners of the green paper with the punch. Punch out three little butterflies and glue in place.

◀ **Paper weaving is extremely easy to do, but is a very effective form of decoration.**

Travel journal

This is an altered book. I purchased a book with unlined pages and carefully removed the cover. Then I re-bound the book using blue card. The card is folded at the sides to create pockets at the front and back of the journal. You can store maps, tickets, photographs and other treasured travel mementoes in these pockets.

YOU WILL NEED

Unlined blank book
  (approx. dimensions
  21 x 15 cm/8¼ x 6 in,
  5 mm/¼ in spine),
  cover removed
PVA (craft) glue
Two 36 cm (14 in)
  lengths narrow white
  ribbon
A3 (297 x 420 mm/
  11¾ x 23½ in) sheet
  blue card
Metal ruler
Pencil
Craft knife
Cutting mat
Embossing tool
Double-sided adhesive
  tape
Map
Scissors
Scrap of light brown
  and dark brown card
Label punch
Stamp stickers

1 Use PVA glue to attach the ends of the narrow ribbon to the book spine. The ribbon should be stuck approximately halfway down the spine, so that it is securely in place. Measure and cut out a length of blue card, 55 x 21 cm (22 x 8½ in).

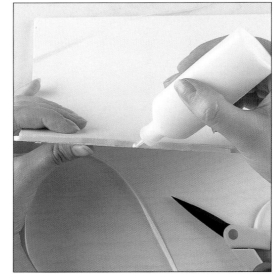

2 Lay the blue card out with the long edge horizontal to you. Find the centre of the long edge, rule a line from long edge to long edge from this point. Lay the spine of the book centrally on this line. Open out the book. On both sides, mark where the card needs to wrap around the book and score. Measure 5 cm (2 in) from the edge of the card on either side and score a line. Fold over on this line and then fold the card around the front and back page of the book. Stick in place with double-sided adhesive tape.

③ Your book is now ready to decorate. Cut out a suitable piece of the map so you have an area measuring 11 x 8.5 cm (4¼ x 3¼ in) and use double-sided tape to attach it in an upper central position on the front of the cover.

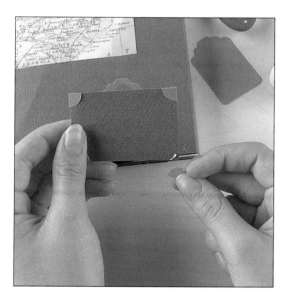

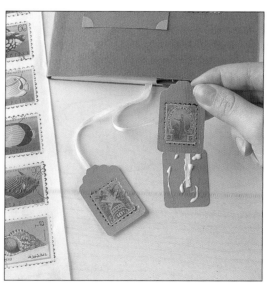

▲ A kitchen journal decorated with pretty gift-wrap. Cut out a few of the illustrations and feature them on the page marker ribbons.

④ Use the template on page 157 to mark and cut out the suitcase from light and dark brown card. Punch out a label shape from light brown coloured card and cut it down to create the handle. Glue the suitcase in place on the bottom left side of the map.

⑤ Punch out four more label shapes. Sandwich two labels at the end of each ribbon and stick a stamp on each label. Stick more stamps on the front cover.

Vintage memories board

This photograph of my grandmother, sister and myself is displayed to good effect, surrounded by vintage bits and bobs that bring back memories of many happy childhood hours spent with my grandmother. The small board in the background shows a different idea with a similar feel.

YOU WILL NEED

Metal ruler

Pencil

Craft knife

Cutting mat

Piece buff-coloured
card 30 x 30 cm
(12 x 12 in)

Suitably decorated
paper handkerchief or
napkin 21 x 21 cm
(8½ x 8½ in)

Aerosol glue

Modge podge™

Photographs or
computer-scanned
images of a selection
of vintage buttons and
sewing materials

Scissors

Decorative scissors

Suitable family
photograph 6 x10 cm
(2½ x 4 in), mounted
on card

4 photo corners

Circle cutter

4 A6 (105 x 148 mm/
4 x 8¼ in) sheets
patterned paper

PVA (craft) glue

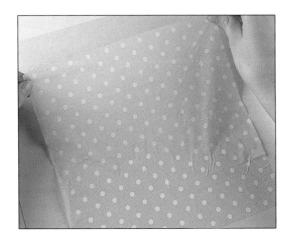

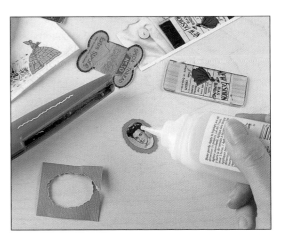

1 The sheet of buff-coloured card will provide the base for your memory board. Tease the layers of the paper handkerchief or napkin apart. It is the top patterned layer that you will be using. Apply aerosol glue to the reverse side of the decorative patterned layer and attach it centrally on the buff base.

2 Prepare your decorative images. Apply Modge podge™ to the images and leave to dry completely (this may take a few hours). Once the Modge podge™ is dry, cut out the images. You may want to leave a narrow border or trim them to the edge. Trim each image as you see fit.

3 Arrange the images as you want them and glue in place. Position the photograph and affix to the board using the photo corners. To create the patchwork corner decoration, use a circle cutter to cut four 6-cm (2½ in) diameter circles from the patterned papers. Cut the circles in half and divide each half into four equal wedges. Use PVA glue to attach them, creating a fan-like patchwork pattern on two corners.

Pricked and embossed wedding sheet

The delicate embossed and pricked decoration is very appropriate for these family wedding photographs. Set on the blue grey card the pattern stands out well.

YOU WILL NEED

Shoot parchment
  15 x 23 cm (6 x 9 in)
Pricking mat
Low-tack adhesive tape
Corner ornamental
  pricking stencil
Embossing tool
Fine pricking tool
Double-sided adhesive
  tape
A4 (210 x 297 mm/
  8¼ x 11¾ in) sheet
  blue-grey thin card
2 photographs, each
  9.5 x 6.5 cm
  (3¾ x 2¾ in)
Decorative scissors

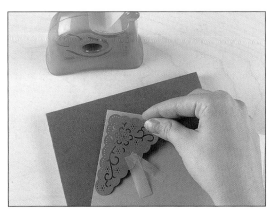

1 Lay the parchment on a pricking mat. Using a short length of low-tack tape, attach the stencil to the top lefthand corner of the parchment. Turn the parchment over so that the stencil is underneath.

2 Run the embossing tool along the lines as marked in the stencil and then begin pricking the remaining pattern. Prick and emboss the pattern in each corner of the parchment, remembering to turn the stencil each time so that the pattern sits correctly in each corner. Use a small part of the stencil design to prick an edging pattern between the corner decorations and add flowers at the top and bottom centre of the parchment.

3 Use double-sided tape to attach the parchment centrally to the sheet of blue-grey card. Trim around the photos with decorative scissors. Use double-sided tape to stick the photographs in place one above the other, centrally on the parchment. Use a paper trimmer to cut a neat border around the parchment sheet.

Family folded photo frame

I chose warm brown colours for this frame to complement the sepia-coloured family photographs. It also makes it look like the commonplace frames are made out of leather or leatherette.

YOU WILL NEED

A3 (297 x 420 mm/ 11¾ x 23¾ in) sheet thin brown card

Pencil

Cutting mat

Metal ruler

Craft knife

Embossing tool

Oval cutter

Scissors

Suitable corner rubber stamp

Embossing pad

Scrap paper

Gold embossing powder

Precision heat tool (see page 13)

Glue stick

Double-sided tape

3 suitable photographs

1 Measure and cut a sheet of brown card 30 x 26 cm (12 x 10¼ in). Keep the offcuts for use in step 2. With the long edge horizontal to you, rule light lines to divide the card into six equal rectangles. Score hill folds along the top two vertical lines. Score valley folds on the central horizontal line and two bottom vertical lines. In each of the top three rectangles, rule lines from corner to corner to find the centre.

2 Cut out an oval measuring 5.5 x 7.5 cm (2¼ x 3 in) in the centre of each of these rectangles. Using the offcuts of brown card, cut out three more ovals the same size. Discard the oval shapes and cut a narrow border around the three oval shaped windows to create frames. Fold the top half of the card down over the bottom half.

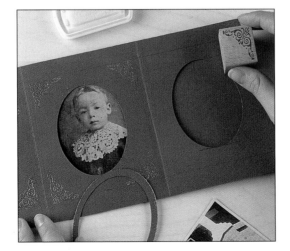

3 Embellish around the oval windows with the stamp. Press the stamp on to the embossing pad and then press on to the card. Working over some scrap paper, sprinkle over the card with embossing powder, shake off the excess then seal with the precision heat tool. Dip the edge of the oval frames into the embossing pad, then into the embossing powder. Shake off the excess and seal with the precision heat tool. Use a glue stick to position the frame around the oval windows. Use double-sided tape to stick the photos in place behind each window. Run glue along the inside of the bottom edges of the card and stick the two edges together.

Floral photo frame

Tissue paper laid over card creates an impression of lightness and adds interesting detail. Either use pink or blue card and paper. The daisies enhance the frame, bringing a little prettiness to it. Try using other punched shapes depending on the photo you have chosen.

YOU WILL NEED

A4 (210 x 297 mm/
  8¼ x 11¾ in) sheet
  white card
Pencil
Metal ruler
Craft knife
Cutting mat
Embossing tool
Punches: disc, daisy
A4 (210 x 297 mm/
  8¼ x 11¾ in) sheet
  blue or pink card
Oval cutter
A4 (210 x 297 mm/
  8¼ x 11¾ in) sheet
  blue or pink decorated
  tissue paper
Aerosol glue
PVA (craft) glue
A5 (148 x 210 mm/
  5¾ x 8¼ in) sheets
  cream and green card
Yellow 3D paint
Family photograph

1 Prepare the photo frame base. Measure and cut out a rectangle 17 x 28.5 cm (6½ x 11¼ in) from the white card. Score and fold in half. Decide which is the back of the card and use a disc punch to cut a half circle from the righthand edge (note that the frame is landscape in shape). Measure and cut out a sheet 17 x 29 cm (6½ x 11½ in) from the blue card. Score and fold the sheet in half. Open up the blue card again. Find the centre of one half of the blue card by ruling two diagonal lines, corner to corner. The spot where the lines cross is the centre. Use the oval cutter to cut an oval 10 x 7.5 cm (4 x 3 in) over the central point you have just made.

2 Use aerosol glue to attach the decorated tissue paper to the blue card. Fold the excess over. Using a craft knife, cut open the tissue paper over the oval cut-out and fold the edges inwards neatly.

▲ **The punched out daisies forming the corner designs are embellished with 3D paint.**

3 Open up the white card with the outer facing you. Spread PVA glue along all of the outer edges of the white card except the edge with the punched out half circle; this is where you will slide your photo into the frame. Carefully place the tissue-covered blue card over the white card. Leave to dry.

4 Punch out 13 cream daisies and 20 green leaves. Use PVA glue to attach the flowers in groups of three around the frame. Glue five leaves around each group of flowers. Embellish the flowers with yellow 3D paint and stick one daisy on the back of the photo frame. Insert the photo into the frame.

Baby photo album

The alphabet-printed vellum pattern is enhanced by the stamped letters inside this little baby album. Choose shades of pink or blue that work well together. Lay all your materials down on the work surface before you begin and choose which letters you will use. You may want to use the baby's name as letters through the book, or possibly different stamped images such as clowns, stars and animals.

YOU WILL NEED

4 A4 (210 x 297 mm/ 8¼ x 11¾ in) sheets thin white card
Craft knife
Cutting mat
Metal ruler
Pencil
Embossing tool
A4 (210 x 297 mm/ 8¼ x 11¾ in) sheet decorated paper for the cover
Aerosol glue
Scissors
Rubber stamps: alphabet and teddy bear
Baby blue stamp pad
35 cm (14 in) thin baby blue ribbon
Double-sided adhesive tape
Suitable photograph for the cover decoration
A5 (148 x 210 mm/ 5¾ x 8¼ in) sheet silver card

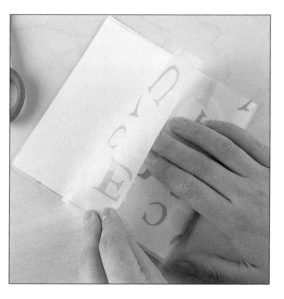

1 Measure and cut out four pieces of thin white card measuring 25 x 13 cm (10 x 5 in). Score and fold the sheets in half. These sheets will form the pages of the album. Measure and cut out a piece of decorated paper 13 x 26 cm (5 x 10½ in). Score and fold in half. Spray the reverse of the decorative paper with aerosol glue and stick to one of the photo album pages. Use scissors to neaten the edges.

2 Pile up the folded pages and cover and mark a point 5 cm (2 in) from the top and bottom. Use scissors to snip small holes in each page and the cover at these marks.

TIP

BEFORE YOU BEGIN MAKING A SPECIAL ALBUM HAVE A LOOK AT THE PHOTOGRAPHS. CONSIDER COLOURS AND MOTIFS AND CHOOSE DECORATIVE PAPER AND STAMPED IMAGES OR STICKERS THAT COMPLEMENT THE PHOTOS. ANOTHER THING TO CONSIDER IS YOUR PERSONAL STYLE. WE ALL DEVELOP STYLES OF OUR OWN, TAKING A LITTLE FROM THIS OR THAT INSPIRATIONAL PICTURE OR PROJECT. IF YOU'RE MAKING THE ALBUM AS A GIFT, CONSIDER THE RECIPIENT. CHOOSE COLOURS AND IMAGES THAT THEY WILL LIKE AND ENJOY.

3 Now you can decorate the pages of your book using the letter and teddy bear stamps. You may want to use letters that make up the baby's name.

4 When you have decorated the pages slip them one inside the other and put the cover around the outside. Thread the ribbon through the holes. Tie in a bow on the outside of the album.

5 To decorate the cover, use double-sided tape to attach your chosen photo to a sheet of silver card. Cut a border around the photo and attach the framed picture to the cover of the album.

Display photo album

This pretty dove grey and parchment decorated album has a delicacy all of its own. The album can be pulled open and displayed on a shelf or bedside table or folded up and tied.

YOU WILL NEED

A2 (420 x 594 mm/
   16½ x 23½ in) sheet
   thin dove grey card
Metal ruler
Pencil
Craft knife
Cutting mat
Embossing tool
Double-sided adhesive
   tape
Grey thread
Scissors
60 cm (24 in) coord-
   inating ribbon 1 cm
   (½ in) wide
PVA (craft) glue
2 A4 (210 x 297 mm/
   8¼ x 11¾ in) sheets
   parchment
Border punch

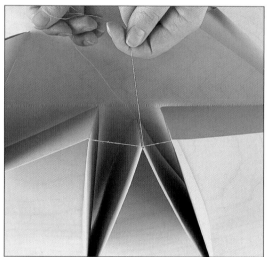

1 Cut out two pieces of grey card 50 x 20 cm (20 x 8 in). Do the following on each piece of card: position the card with the longest edge horizontal to you. Rule a light pencil line across the centre of the card. Score a valley fold. Divide the card into eight equal rectangles. Score the top three lines – hill fold, valley fold, hill fold. Do the same on the three bottom lines, but this time start with a valley fold. Fold the top half of the card over the bottom half. Cut out a piece of grey card 9 x 2.5 cm (3½ x1 in). Score to fold the cut piece lengthways. Use this piece of grey card to join the two folded sheets together. Place double-sided tape along the front of the piece and slip between the joins. Use double-sided tape to join on the reverse in the same manner. You should now have a long concertina of card as shown below.

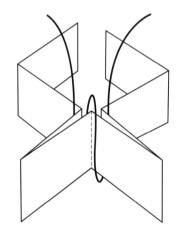

2 Place the project upright in a star position on the work surface. Referring to the photo and diagram above, use a length of thread to hold the centre together, knotting the thread in place.

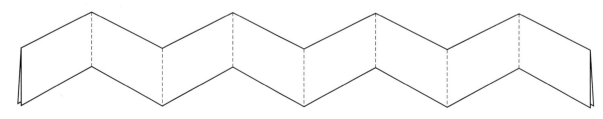

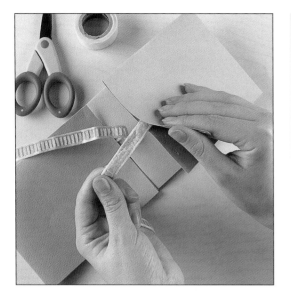

③ Cut the length of ribbon in half and attach a piece to each end, in between the card layers, with PVA glue.

④ To decorate the album you will need eight strips of parchment cut to a width of 3 cm (1¼ in). Use the border punch to decorate both edges of each strip. Use PVA glue to stick the borders at the edge of each 'page', on the side that is going to be visible when the album is displayed.

▼ **This pretty single photo frame has been created using a corner punch and making a double cut at each corner to hold the photo.**

⑤ To make the photo corners use 5 mm (¼ in) wide lengths of parchment 3 cm (1¼ in) long. Fold centrally at right angles to form corners and hold in place with double-sided tape. Slip the corner on to the photos, peel away the protective layer on the double-sided tape and stick in place centrally on the page.

Fringed flower bag

These flowers are made from coiled strips of fringed paper. They look like asters to me, soft and pretty. I have chosen a turquoise, violet and purple colour scheme, but other colours would work equally well. The flowers would look just as good decorating a gift box or greeting card.

YOU WILL NEED

A3 (297 x 420 mm/
   11¾ x 23½ in) sheet
   thin turquoise card
Metal ruler
Pencil
Embossing tool
Craft knife
Cutting mat
Glue stick
Decorative paper
   fasteners: 4 yellow
   and 3 blue
A5 (148 x 210 mm/
   5¾ x 8¼ in) sheets
   violet and purple
   paper
Bulldog clip
Scissors
Quilling tool
PVA (craft) glue
A5 (148 x 210 mm/
   5¾ x 8¼ in) sheets
   yellow and turquoise
   card

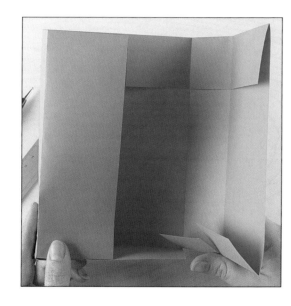

1 Use the guide on page 159 to construct the bag out of the turquoise card. Use a glue stick to hold the folds in place. (Keep the offcuts of card for use later.) To make the handle, cut a strip of card 2 cm wide (¾ in) and 20 cm (8 in) long. Use two paper fasteners to attach the handle to the bag.

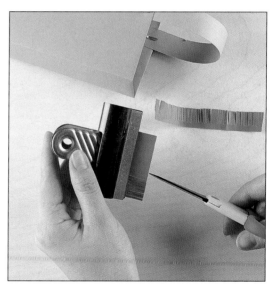

2 To construct the flowers cut strips from the violet and purple paper measuring 1.5 cm (⅝ in) wide and 10 cm (4 in) long. You will need five flowers – three violet and two purple. Fold the strip in half and set 5 mm (¼ in) into the bulldog clip. Use scissors to snip up to the clip edge, thereby creating a fringe.

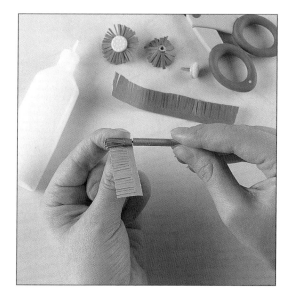

③ Take your quilling tool and slip on to one end of the prepared fringed paper. Coil the paper. When it is completely coiled release slightly and glue the un-fringed end. Push a paper fastener through the fringes and through the hole. Splay out the fringe to create the flower petals. Make all of the flowers in this way.

④ Prepare the woven decoration. Cut an 8 cm (3¼ in) square of turquoise card. Draw three light pencil lines across the square – one across the middle and two 5 mm (¼ in) in from each side. Cut along these lines with a craft knife, stopping short of the edge on both sides.

⑤ Cut two strips of yellow card 3 cm (1¼ in) wide and 8 cm (3¼ in) long. Weave the yellow strips through the turquoise card to create a chequerboard effect.

⑥ Attach a flower to each square, pushing the paper fasteners through the card. Glue the decoration to the front of the bag. Make a label from a 6-cm (2½ in) square of yellow card, attach a flower and hang the tag from the bag handle.

Paper dolly gift-wrap

This colourful gift-wrap is fun and easy to make and would be wonderful to wrap around a child's gift. The matching card is a nice added touch.

YOU WILL NEED

8 A5 (148 x 210 mm/
  5¾ x 8¼ in) sheets
  white paper
Pencil
Scissors
Patterned paper for
  the dresses
A4 (210 x 297 mm/
  8¼ x 11¾ in) sheet
  brown paper
Glue stick
A2 (420 x 594 mm/
  16½ x 23½ in) sheet
  green paper

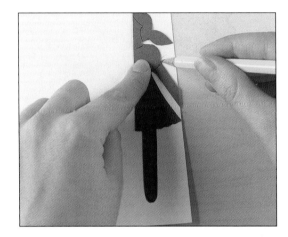

1 Lay the half-dolly template (see page 157) on one end of a sheet of white paper exactly as shown above. Draw around the template.

2 Using the fold line indicated on the template, fold the sheet of paper into a concertina shape. Cut through the concertina folds. Open out and you should have a row of paper dolls. Repeat with the other sheets of white paper.

3 Fold pieces of card and patterned paper from which to cut the hair and dress (see page 157). Lay the edges of the templates on the fold lines of the card and paper. Draw around the templates then cut out. Cut enough to 'dress' all of the dolls.

4 Use a glue stick to attach the dresses and hair to the dolls. Cut one doll off the end of a row to make the matching card. Stick the rows of dressed dolls on to the sheet of green paper.

Embossed daisy bag

Here I have created my own embossing stencil. Have a look through your punches and see what other images you could use as embossed shapes.

YOU WILL NEED

A3 (297 x 420 mm/
  11¾ x 23½ in) sheet
  thin pink card
Craft knife
Metal ruler
Cutting mat
PVA (craft) glue
Daisy punch
A5 (148 x 210 mm/
  5¾ x 8¼ in) sheet white
  card
A5 (148 x 210 mm/
  5¾ x 8¼ in) sheet
  embossing parchment
Embossing tool
Scissors

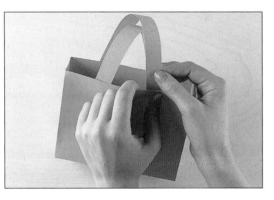

1 Make the bag from thin pink card, using the guide on page 156. Hold the folds in place with PVA glue. To make the bag handles cut two strips of pink card 28 x 2 cm (11 x ¾ in). Attach the handles centrally on the bag, crossing them over.

2 Now that the bag has been made you can make up the embossing pattern. You will need a daisy punch and a sheet of A5 white card. Cut two 5 cm (2 in) squares of white card and punch a daisy shape in the centre of each square. Use PVA glue to stick the punched squares exactly on top of one another. Use the template on page 156 and a craft knife to cut out the leaf and stem shapes from a single layer of white card.

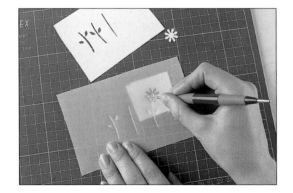

3 Emboss a design on to a piece of parchment measuring 13.5 x 9.5 cm (5 x 3¾ in) using the embossing tool and your templates. Cut a 13.5 x 9.5 cm (5 x 3¾ in) piece of pink card. Cut a 10 x 6.5 cm (4 x 2½ in) window out of the card.

4 Use PVA glue to attach the embossed parchment centrally on the front of the bag. Attach the frame to the decorated parchment. Finally, embellish the frame with narrow ribbons of parchment and punched daisies.

Ballerina bag

What better wrapping for a little girl's gift than pink frills, stars and sparkle? You could make a card to go with the bag, using the same motif.

YOU WILL NEED

A3 (297 x 420 mm/
    11¾ x 23½ in) sheet
    white card
Craft knife
Metal ruler
Cutting mat
Embossing tool
PVA (craft) glue
Pink tissue paper
A4 (210 x 297 mm/
    8¼ x 11¾ in) sheet
    pink paper
Pink gel pen
3D sticky foam pads
Glitter stars in silver
    and pink
Silver glitter
Scrap of silver card
Star stickers
Short length ribbon for
    the gift-tag

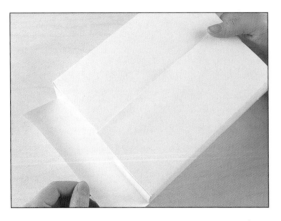

1 Use the guide on page 159 to construct the bag from white card. Use PVA glue to secure the folds. For the handles cut two strips of white card, 22 x 1.5 cm (8½ x ½ in) and two strips of silver 22 x 0.5 cm (8½ x ⅕in). Glue the silver strips in the centre of the white. Attach the handles.

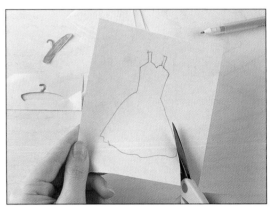

2 Using the templates on page 158 cut out three pink tissue paper tutus. Cut the following out of pink paper: one tutu, one bodice, three stars and one coathanger. Colour in the coathanger with pink gel pen before you cut it out.

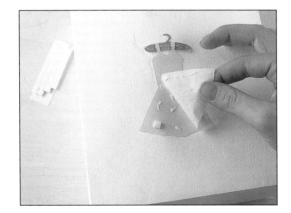

3 Use PVA glue to attach the coathanger, the bodice and pink card tutu in the centre of the front of the bag. Layer on the tissue paper tutus, sticking them with glue plus a few 3D sticky foam pads. Decorate the dress with pink gel pen and glitters. Cut a tiny strip of silver card for the wand. Stick in place, topped with a star sticker.

4 Cut four narrow strips of silver card and pink paper approx. 14 cm (5½ in) long and frame the dress with them. Embellish the frame with the two pink stars. Make up a tag from white card, 6 x 4 cm (2½ x 1½ in). Stick a pink star in the centre and attach a silver star sticker. Attach to the bag handle with ribbon.

Galleries

THREE-DIMENSIONAL ELEMENTS

Japanese Kimono Card (1)

Attach a kimono peel-off to pink paper then cut out. Use felt-tips to colour the pattern on the kimono. Create a border with strips of gold card. Fold a rectangle of paper into a concertina to make the fan. Cut the little sandals out of card.

By the Seaside Card (2)

Cut three sandcastle shapes and use 3D sticky foam pads to hold them in place. Use sequins for the shells and draw the red flag and spade freehand on to card, then cut out. Cut small triangles from stripy paper for the bunting. Cut the seagulls from scraps of white paper.

Sushi Card (3)

I love this card – quilling is the perfect method for constructing sushi shapes. Quill the white rice shape first then surround it with a black quilled strip. Use 3D paint to decorate the sushi. Cut the chopsticks from brown card and attach them using 3D sticky foam pads.

Romantic Rose Card (4)

Construct a simple small ring box and lid using red card. Stick in place with 3D sticky foam pads. Cut little slits to slip the silver card ring band through; use a gem sticker for the stone. Embellish the ring box and corners of the motif with silver hearts and use a single red rose sticker to finish the design.

Witches Card (5)

Cut a simple skyline out of black card. Use a yellow marker pen to create an impression of glass in the windows. Use a circle cutter to cut a disc out of yellow card to create the full moon. Punch out three witches on broomsticks from black card and attach using 3D sticky foam pads.

Valentine Gift Box (6)

Construct a box using green card and create the ribbon effect using strips of white paper. Make the flowers following the instructions on pages 76–78.

These pop-ups are made using the technique shown on page 19.

Baby's Pram (1)
Use the pram shape on page 64. Attach the pram to a central elbow, and the flowers to two smaller elbows.

Simple Valentine (2)
Cut a heart shape from red paper and used double-sided tape to attach it to gold card. Trim around the edges with decorative scissors.

Birthday Cake (3)
The perfect birthday card – increase or decrease the number of candles to suit the recipient. Cut the cake from pastel-coloured card and glue the cake together before attaching it to the pop-up elbow. Create a background using patterned paper, peel-offs or stickers.

Through the Window (4)
This card works from the outside as well as the inside. Cut out the window shape. Decorate the front cover of the card with a line of flowers under the window. The sideboard is made up of brown card rectangles. Make up the vase using an oval shape and punch out little flowers to fill it. Cut the curtain shapes from coloured paper and use a cat peel-off or sticker.

In the Garden (5)
Cut motifs from a sheet of appropriate wrapping paper. Construct a row of pop-up elbows and stick an image to each one. This gives an impression of a garden.

CREATING MOTIFS

Christmas Lights Card (1)

The green background gives the impression of a Christmas tree. Use a leaf punch to cut the lightbulb shapes from translucsent coloured paper. Glue them along drawn pen lines, then paint a dot of green 3D paint at the top of each shape. Embellish with star stickers.

Paper Lanterns Card (2)

The violet blue card base works well with the pink lanterns and pale blue hydrangea-like flowers. Construct the lanterns from discs of ridged pink card. Glue narrow strips of black card at the top and bottom of each disc. Punch simple flower shapes from thin blue card and place in groups.

Shopping Gift Bag Card (3)

Construct a bag out of thin blue card. To make the handbag, punch out a luggage label shape, bend over the top and stick with 3D sticky foam pads. Draw the umbrella freehand and cut out of red card. Attach with 3D sticky foam pads. Find shoe and heart peel-offs, and the bunch of flowers is punched from thin red card and embellished with gold 3D paint.

Halloween Card (4)

Cut the cobweb from a scrap of mulberry paper and use the template on page 155 to cut the bats out of black card. The glasses containing green liquid are punched from parchment and green card. Draw the candlabra shape in green 3D glitter paint onto a black base. Cut the candles from white card and draw the flame with yellow 3D paint. Use 3D tape to attach the candleabra on the table. The pumpkin is a peel-off and make the broom using a quilled fringe stuck to a strip of brown card.

Sunflowers Card (5)

Punch lots of daisy shapes out of varying shades and textures of yellow card. To make each sunflower layer three daisies together. Glue them in a staggered fashion to give an impression of lots of petals. Punch the flower centres out of brown card. Cut out a vase shape. Create the background to the vase of flowers from two different coloured cards. Run a line of red card across to create a feeling of depth.

Valentine Gift Box (6)

The decoration on this box is simple yet very effective. Construct a simple box from red card. Attach two strips of gold paper across the box. Punch hearts from thin red card and gold paper and layer together. Attach the hearts along the strips of gold paper using 3D sticky foam pads. Decorate the lid of the box with little peel-off flower stickers.

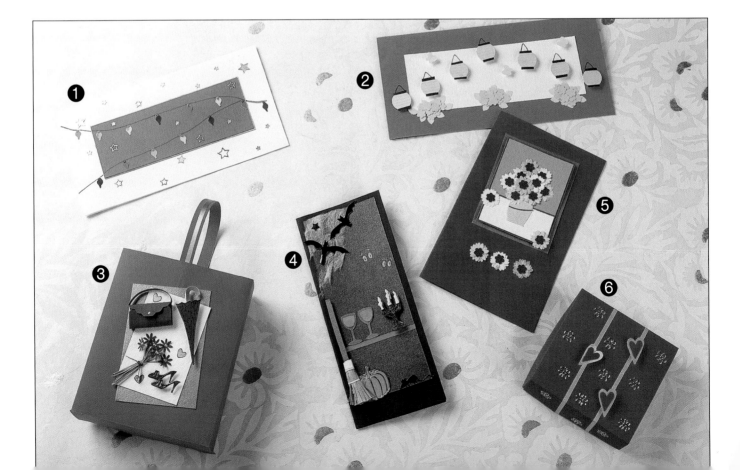

Naughty Kitty Card (1)

Stick the feature peel-off to thin black card and cut around it. Stick the motif to the folded card blank. Stick a strip of red paper across the front of the card, around to the back. Stick strips of blue paper across the front and back of the card and inside, to give the impression of shelves. Stick black paw print stickers across the front and inside the card.

Icecream Sundae Card (2)

Cut pastel-coloured circular shapes from card to create balls of ice cream. Pile them on top of one another. Stick to a sheet of green card and cut out a sundae glass shape and shape the top around the ice cream. Cut a sundae glass shape out of parchment and shade using an embossing tool. Stick the parchment on top of the green sundae glass. Stick this onto a folded sheet of white card, with the top of the sundae on the fold. Cut around the sundae to create your card, not cutting right across the top, to create your card.

Flower Seller Card (3)

Fold an A5 (148 x 219 mm/5¾ x 8¼ in) sheet of white card in half. Cut a rectangle of orange card for the barrow and stick on the card blank, up to the fold. Cut out the wheels and edge them with embossing powder. Punch flowers from orange and yellow card and leaves from green card. Stick on top of the barrow, working up to the fold. Cut around the barrow shape. Decorate the flowers with 3D paint.

Witch's Hat Gift Bag (4)

Make a simple bag from thin black card and embellish with silver glitter glue dots. Cut a witch's hat out of black card. Embellish with silver marker and silver glitter glue and hang from handle.

Sailing Boats Card (5)

This concertina-shaped card is constructed from thin blue card and the boats are from a paper table napkin. The punched silver dolphins and strips of blue tissue paper add to the nautical air.

Templates and diagrams

All templates are shown at 100% unless otherwise stated.
Solid lines should be cut. Dashed lines should be scored and folded.

Keepsake box (pages 30–32)

These are reference diagrams to be used as a guide; they are not drawn to actual size.

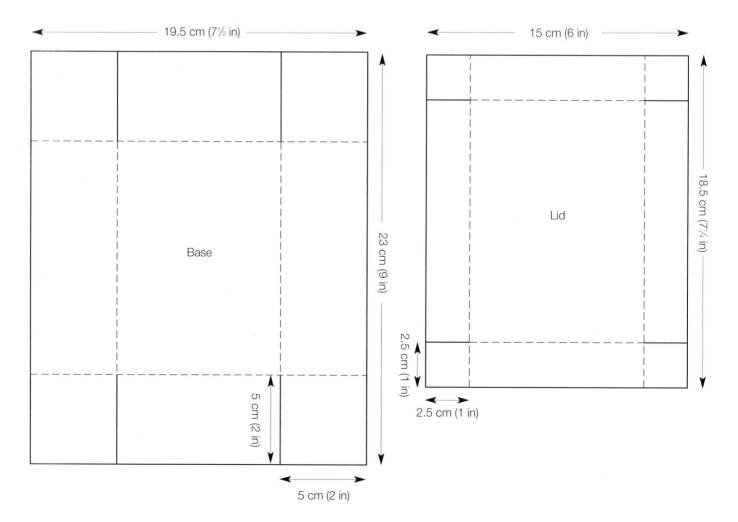

19.5 cm (7½ in)

Base

23 cm (9 in)

5 cm (2 in)

5 cm (2 in)

15 cm (6 in)

Lid

18.5 cm (7¼ in)

2.5 cm (1 in)

2.5 cm (1 in)

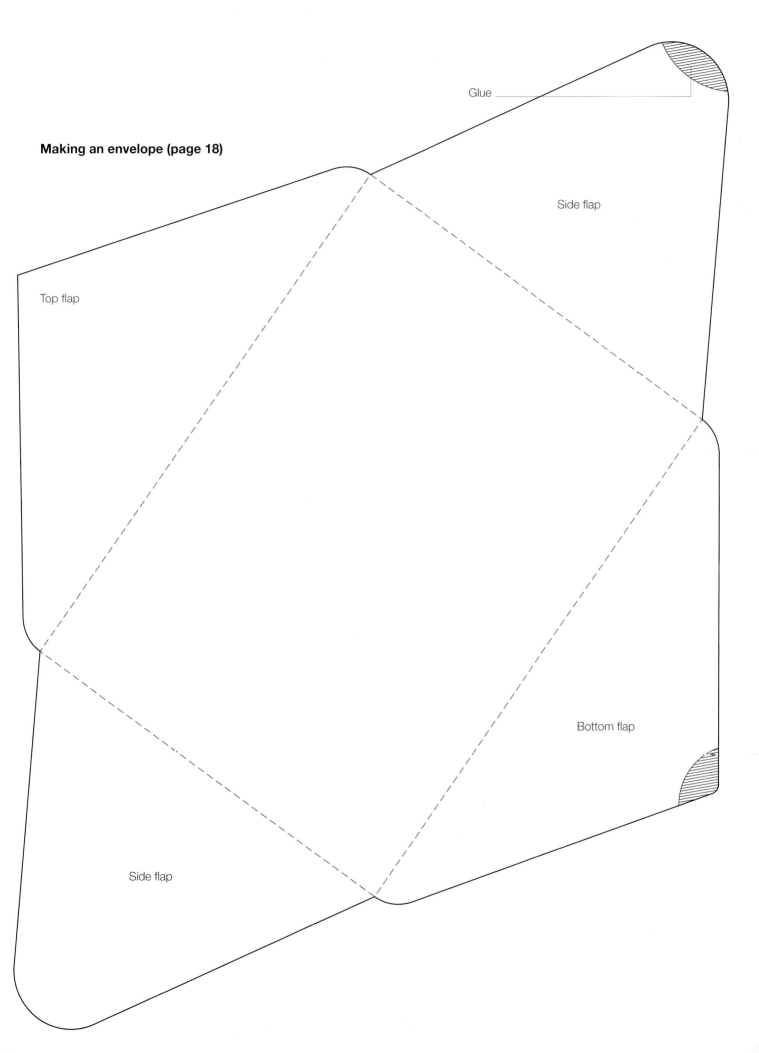

Making an envelope (page 18)

Glue

Side flap

Top flap

Bottom flap

Side flap

Daisy boxes (pages 39–41)

The diagrams for the box base and lid are reference diagrams to be used as a guide; they are not drawn to actual size.

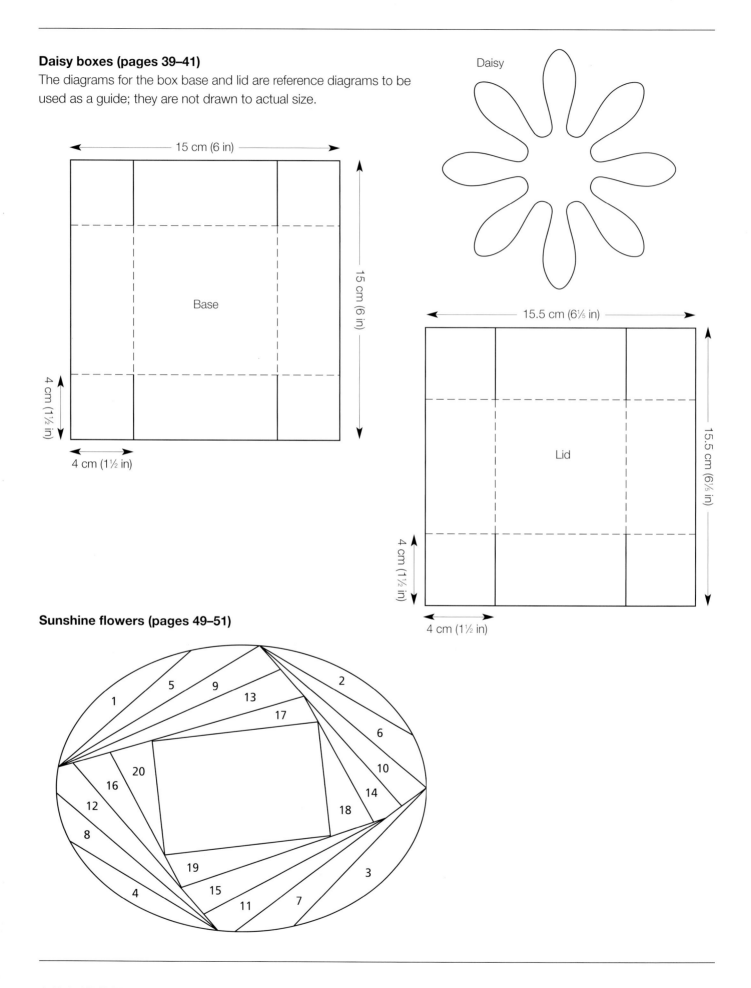

Daisy

15 cm (6 in)

15 cm (6 in)

Base

4 cm (1½ in)

4 cm (1½ in)

15.5 cm (6⅛ in)

15.5 cm (6⅛ in)

Lid

4 cm (1½ in)

4 cm (1½ in)

Sunshine flowers (pages 49–51)

Little cut and fold box (see pages 42–43)

The diagrams for the box base and lid are shown at half actual size. You will need to photocopy them at 200%

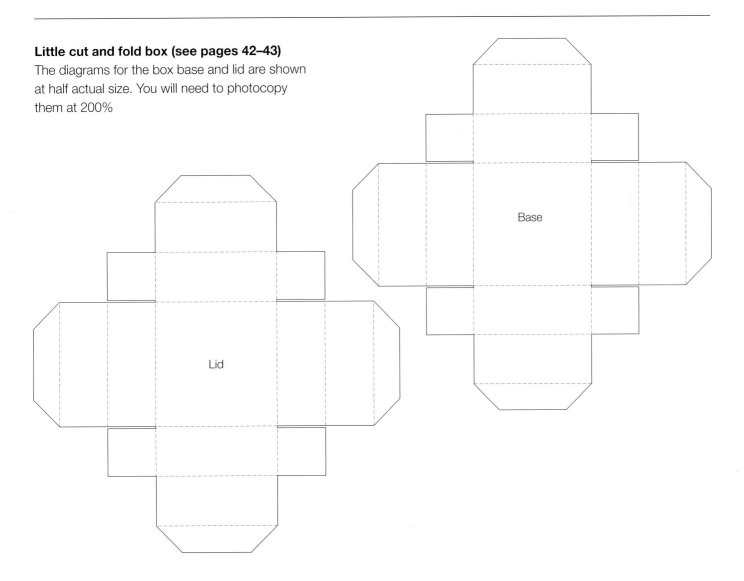

Base

Lid

Easter eggs in a woven basket (pages 55–57)

Basket

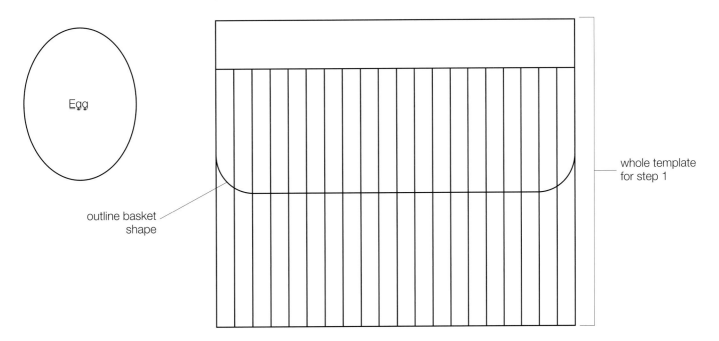

Egg

whole template for step 1

outline basket shape

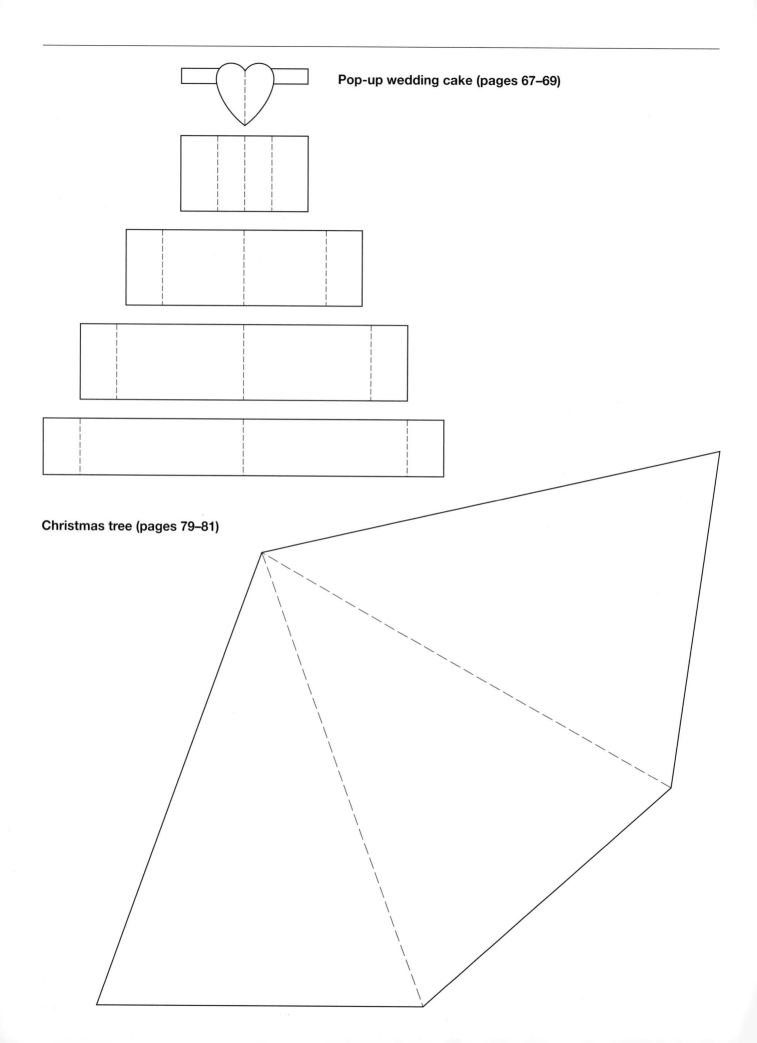

Pop-up wedding cake (pages 67–69)

Christmas tree (pages 79–81)

Lucky black cats (pages 82–85)

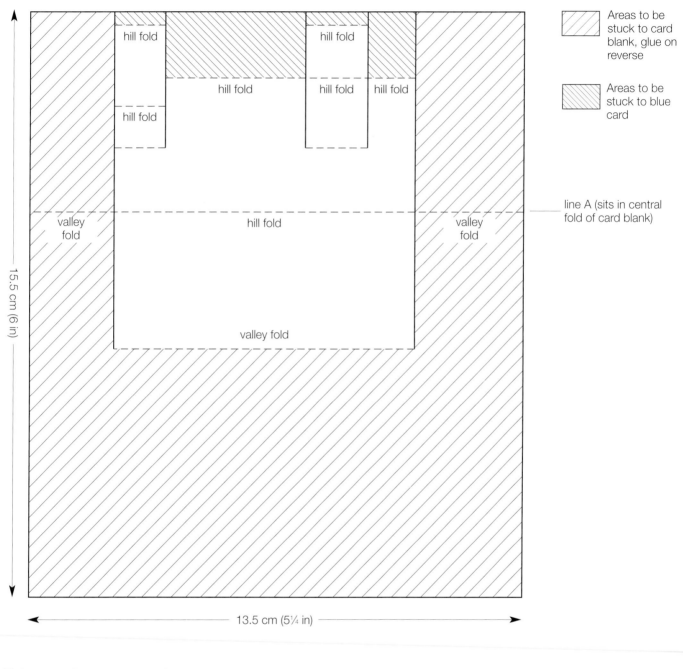

hill fold

hill fold

hill fold

hill fold

hill fold

hill fold

hill fold

valley fold

hill fold

valley fold

valley fold

15.5 cm (6 in)

13.5 cm (5¼ in)

Areas to be stuck to card blank, glue on reverse

Areas to be stuck to blue card

line A (sits in central fold of card blank)

Halloween (pages 100–101)

Bat

Pumpkins

Three apple trees (pages 86–87)

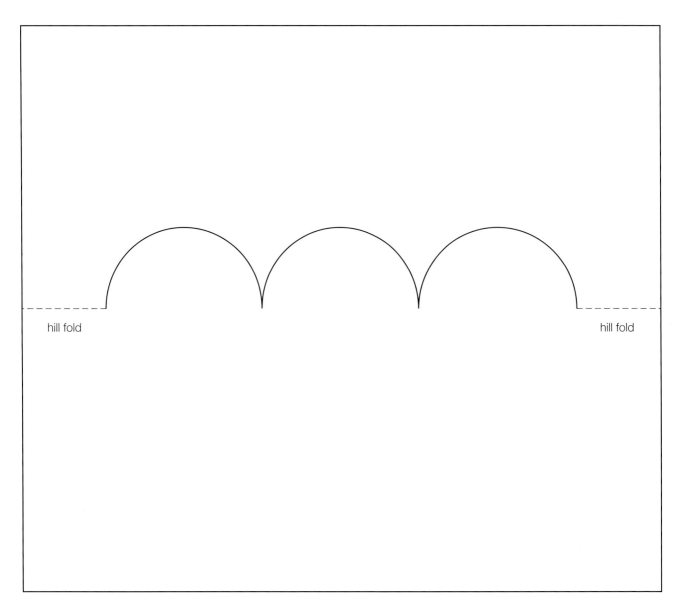

hill fold

hill fold

Embossed daisy bag (pages 142–143)
Diagram for bag to be used as a guide; it is
not drawn to actual size.

Flower stalks and leaves

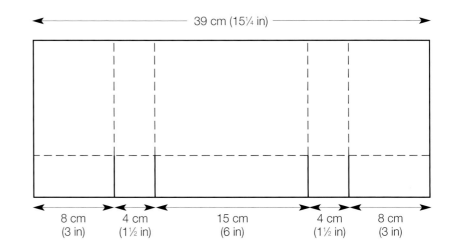

39 cm (15¼ in)

| 8 cm (3 in) | 4 cm (1½ in) | 15 cm (6 in) | 4 cm (1½ in) | 8 cm (3 in) |

Wedding place settings (page 96)

Daisy bookmark (pages 107–109)

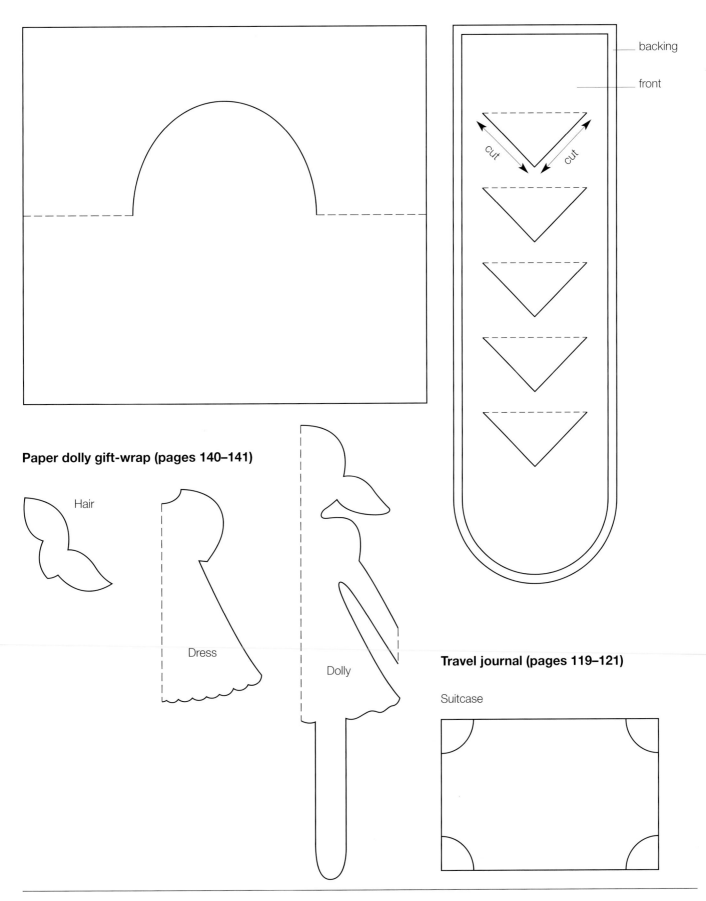

backing

front

cut

cut

Paper dolly gift-wrap (pages 140–141)

Hair

Dress

Dolly

Travel journal (pages 119–121)

Suitcase

Kimono doll mobile (pages 110–112)

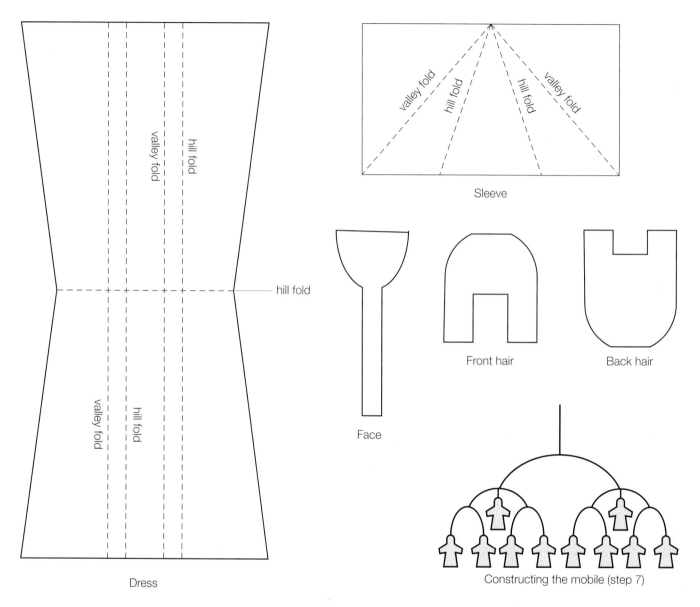

valley fold

hill fold

hill fold

valley fold

hill fold

Dress

valley fold · hill fold · hill fold · valley fold

Sleeve

Face

Front hair

Back hair

Constructing the mobile (step 7)

Ballerina bag (pages 144–145)

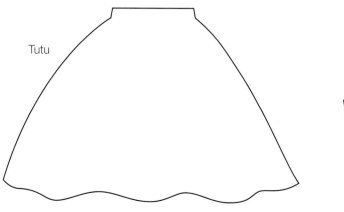

Tutu

Bodice

Fringed flower bag (137–139)

This is a reference diagram to be used
as a guide; it is not drawn to actual size.

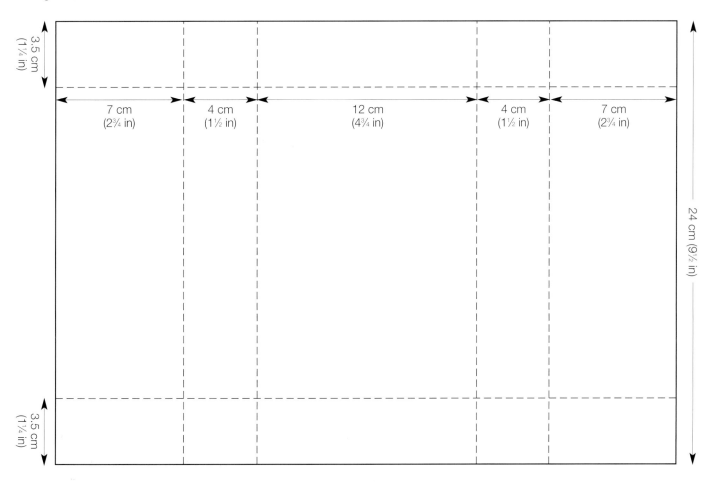

3.5 cm
(1¼ in)

7 cm
(2¾ in)

4 cm
(1½ in)

12 cm
(4¾ in)

4 cm
(1½ in)

7 cm
(2¾ in)

24 cm (9½ in)

3.5 cm
(1¼ in)

Ballerina bag (pages 144–145) Bag diagram is for reference; not drawn to actual size.

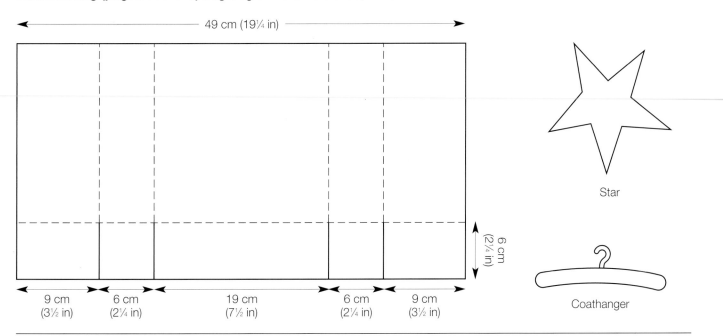

49 cm (19¼ in)

6 cm
(2¼ in)

9 cm
(3½ in)

6 cm
(2¼ in)

19 cm
(7½ in)

6 cm
(2¼ in)

9 cm
(3½ in)

Star

Coathanger

Index